BEST-KEPT SECRETS OF
EUROPE

Publisher and Creative Director: Nick Wells
Assistant Editor and Picture Research: Josie Mitchell
Art Director and Layout Design: Mike Spender
Copy Editor: Ramona Lamport
Proofreader: Dawn laker

Special thanks to: Laura Bulbeck

FLAME TREE PUBLISHING
6 Melbray Mews,
Fulham, London SW6 3NS
United Kingdom

www.flametreepublishing.com

First published 2015

15 17 19 18 16
1 3 5 7 9 10 8 6 4 2

Courtesy of Shutterstock.com and © the following contributors: maziarz 12; R.rrainbow 13, 15; ErickN 14; Pigprox 16; Matthew Jacques 17; vvoe
18; Netfalls - Remy Musser 20; andersphoto 21; ivan bastien 22; Christian Mueller 24, 28; chrisdorney 25; TTstudio 27, 29, 108; Cedric Weber 30;
Liubov Terletska 31; PlusONE 32, 36; osmera.com 33; Roberaten 34; Brendan Howard 37; Shaiith 38; Nataliya Hora 39; Claudio Divizia 40;
Heartland Arts 41; Patrik Dietrich 42; Semmick Photo 44; M Reel 45; Aitormmfoto 46; VanderWolf Images 47; Rob Wilson 48, 83; Lauren Orr 50;
CristinaMuraca 51; Leonid Andronov 52; pisaphotography 53; Kemal Taner 54; SP-Photo 55; Rudolf Tepfenhart 56; Jule_Berlin 57; Christian Draghici
58; Anibal Trejo 60; Mario Savoia 61; Steven Bostock 62; Giancarlo Liguori 63; Artur Bogacki 64; Brian Kinney 68, 114; Fly_dragonfly 69; J2R 70;
Sergey Kelin 72; Iakov Filimonov 73; Luciano Mortula 74, 152; peresanz 76; bright 77; Vitalez 78; Arseniy Krasnevsky 80; Genova 81; Eric Crama 82;
Eva Madrazo 84; AdrianNunez 85; KarSol 86; Gubin Yury 88; Vlada Z 89; Rob van Esch 90; Giacomo Pratellesi 91; Mihai-Bogdan Lazar 92;
Nick_Nick 96, 102; Catarina Belova 97; JeniFoto 98; Santi Rodriguez 99; photka 100; Alexander Demyanenko 103; Frank Bach 104; Oleg Senkov
106; maurizio 107; naten 110; Malgorzata Kistryn 111; Wolfgang Zwanzger 112; alech 115; nito 116; trotalo 117; clearlens 118; Mikadun 119; Alessio
Moiola 120; Dmitri Ometsinsky 122; Kushch Dmitry 123; Ivana Zelenakova 124; Oleg Znamenskiy 125; canadastock 126, 185; irakite 128, 138; Emi
Cristea 130; Khirman Vladimir 131; S.Borisov 132; Anastasios71 133, 137; littlewormy 134; PavleMarjanovic 136; lornet 139, 147; vitmark 140;
Dariusz Majgier 141; Scorpp 142; Constantin Stanciu 143; Roman Sulla 144; Ochkin Alexey 146; Serg Zastavkin 148; ihsan Gercelman 149; Sailorr
150; saiko3p 153; Tatiana Popova 154; AlxYago 155; Vincent St. Thomas 156; OPIS Zagreb 157; Premysl 160; l i g h t p o e t 161; Kajano 162;
Famed01 164; Mikhail Markovskiy 165; graphia 166; Capture Light 167; GoneWithTheWind 168; QQ7 169; Alexander Mazurkevich 170, 175;
posztos 171; takepicsforfun 173; Neirfy 174; Sergey Novikov 176; InavanHateren 177; Anton_Ivanov 178; Lisa S. 179; mRGB 180; Elena Schweitzer
181; Tupungato 182; SergeiSki 184; Renata Sedmakova 186; Alexander Tolstykh 187; Anton Gvozdikov 188.

ISBN 978-1-78361-606-0

Printed in China

BEST-KEPT SECRETS OF
EUROPE

GORDON KERR

**FLAME TREE
PUBLISHING**

CONTENTS

INTRODUCTION   6

WESTERN EUROPE   10
Notre Dame, Paris, France   12
Parc Montsouris, Paris, France   13
Château de Vincennes, Paris, France   14
Café at Rue Mouffetard, Paris, France   15
The Louvre, Paris, France   16
Musée de l'Orangerie, Paris, France   17
Saint-Sulpice Church and Fountain,
   Paris, France   18
Eiffel Tower, Paris, France   20
Passage des Panoramas, Paris, France   21
Montmartre, Paris, France   22
Portobello Road, London, England   24
Peter Pan Statue, Kensington Gardens,
   London, England   25
St Paul's Cathedral, London, England   26
Kew Gardens, London, England   28
Tower Bridge, London, England   29
Leadenhall Market, London, England   30
The Sherlock Holmes Museum,
   London, England   31

The Italian Gardens, Kensington
   Gardens, London, England   32
National Maritime Museum,
   Greenwich, London, England   33
Big Ben and the Houses of Parliament,
   London, England   34
Scott Monument, Edinburgh, Scotland   36
St Giles Cathedral, Edinburgh, Scotland   37
Arthur's Seat and Edinburgh Cityscape,
   Edinburgh, Scotland   38
The Scotch Whisky Experience,
   Edinburgh, Scotland   39
Edinburgh Castle, Edinburgh, Scotland   40
Dean Gallery, Edinburgh, Scotland   41
Leith Harbour, Edinburgh, Scotland   42
Wellington Monument, Phoenix Park,
   Dublin, Ireland   44
Lake at Farmleigh, Dublin, Ireland   45
Temple Bar, Dublin, Ireland   46
Plato Sculpture, Trinity College Library,
   Dublin, Ireland   47
The Samuel Beckett Bridge,
   Dublin, Ireland   48
Christ Church Cathedral, Dublin, Ireland   50
Stephen's Green Shopping Centre,
   Dublin, Ireland   51
Berlin Cathedral, Berlin, Germany   52
The Cupola on top of the Reichstag
   Building, Berlin, Germany   53
Haus der Kulturen der Welt, Berlin, Germany   54
Tiergarten, Berlin, Germany   55
Charlottenburg Palace, Berlin, Germany   56
Berlin Wall, Berlin, Germany   57
The Oberbaum Bridge, Berlin, Germany   58
Rijksmuseum, Amsterdam, The Netherlands   60
Tulips, Amsterdam Flower Market,
   Amsterdam, The Netherlands   61

Anne Frank Statue, near the Anne Frank
   Museum, Amsterdam, The Netherlands   62
The Modern EYE Film Institute by the IJ
   Harbour, Amsterdam, The Netherlands   63
Singel Canal, Amsterdam, The Netherlands   64

THE IBERIAN PENINSULA   66
Gaudi's Casa Batlló, Barcelona, Spain   68
Parc del Laberint d'Horta, Barcelona, Spain   69
Barcelona Beach, Barcelona, Spain   70
La Boqueria Market, Barcelona, Spain   72
Restaurants at Plaça Reial, Barcelona, Spain   73
Parc Güell, Barcelona, Spain   74
Carrer del Bisbe, Gothic Quarter,
   Barcelona, Spain   76
Arc de Triomf, Barcelona, Spain   77
The Centre of Barcelona, Barcelona, Spain   78
Museu Nacional d'Art de Catalunya,
   Barcelona, Spain   80
Gaudi Chimney at Casa Milà, Barcelona, Spain   81
Sobrino de Botín Restaurant, Madrid, Spain   82
Cibeles Fountain, Madrid, Spain   83

Reina Sofia Museum, Madrid, Spain   84
Crystal Palace in Retiro Park, Madrid, Spain   85
The Royal Palace, Madrid, Spain   86
Rossio Square, Baixa District, Lisbon, Portugal 88
Historical House in Alfama, Lisbon, Portugal   89
Trams on Bica Funicular, near Bairro Alto,
       Lisbon, Portugal   90
Queluz National Palace, Lisbon, Portugal   91
Jerónimos Monastery, Lisbon, Portugal   92

ITALY AND THE MEDITERRANEAN   **94**
Colosseum, Rome, Italy   96
Street in Trastevere, Rome, Italy   97
Ancient Roman Ruins of a Bakery,
       Ostia Antica, Rome, Italy   98
Hadrian's Villa, Rome, Italy   99
St Peter's Square, Rome, Italy   100
Trevi Fountain, Rome, Italy   102
The Spanish Steps, Rome, Italy   103
Temple of Esculapio, Villa Borghese,
       Rome, Italy   104
Colossus Statue of Constantine
       the Great, Rome, Italy   106
Pyramid of Cestius, Rome, Italy   107
Panorama of the Vatican City, Rome, Italy   108
The Great Synagogue, Florence, Italy   110
Bardini Garden and view of Florence,
       Florence, Italy   111
San Frediano in Cestello Church,
       Florence, Italy   112
Basilica di Santa Croce, Florence, Italy   114
Uffizi Gallery, Florence, Italy   115
Palazzo Pitti, Florence, Italy   116
The Fountain of Neptune, Florence, Italy   117
Boboli Garden, Florence, Italy   118
Santa Maria del Fiore Cathedral, Florence, Italy 119
The Ponte Vecchio on the River Arno,
       Florence, Italy   120
Piazza San Marco, Venice, Italy   122
The Art Blue Café in Campo Santo
       Stefano, Venice, Italy   123

Scala Contarini del Bovolo, Venice, Italy   124
Rialto Bridge, Venice, Italy   125
Grand Canal, Venice, Italy   126
Dorsoduro Neighbourhood, Venice, Italy   128
Church of Panaghia Kapnikarea, Athens,
       Greece   130
Theatre of Dionysus, Athens, Greece   131
Acropolis of Athens, Athens, Greece   132
Pittaki Street, Athens, Greece   133
Mikrolimano Marina in Piraeus,
       Athens, Greece   134
Parthenon, Athens, Greece   136
Athens National Garden, Athens, Greece   137
Anafiotika, Plaka, Athens, Greece   138
Mount Lycabettus, Athens, Greece   139
Monastery in Messara Valley, Crete, Greece   140
Lefka Ori Mountains, Crete, Greece   141
Knossos Palace, Crete, Greece   142
Samaria Gorge, Crete, Greece   143
Agios Nikolaos, Crete, Greece   144
Monastery of Arkadi Garden, Crete, Greece   146
Matala Beach and Caves, near Heraklion,
       Crete, Greece   147
Medusa Column in the Basilica Cistern,
       Istanbul, Turkey   148
Süleymaniye Mosque, Istanbul, Turkey   149
The Bosphorus Bridge, Istanbul, Turkey   150
Sultan Ahmed Mosque, Istanbul, Turkey   152
The Grand Bazaar, Istanbul, Turkey   153
Hagia Sophia, Istanbul, Turkey   154
Dolmabahçe Clock Tower, Istanbul, Turkey   155
Rumeli Fortress, Istanbul, Turkey   156
Chora Church, Istanbul, Turkey   157

CENTRAL AND EASTERN EUROPE   **158**
Vrtbovská Garden, Prague, Czech Republic   160
Charles Bridge, Prague, Czech Republic   161
Prague Castle, Prague, Czech Republic   162
Franz Kafka Statue in the Jewish Quarter,
       Prague, Czech Republic   164
Jubilee Synagogue, Prague, Czech Republic   165

Havel's Market, Prague, Czech Republic   166
Chapel of the Holy Sepulchre on
       Pet ín Hill, Prague, Czech Republic   167
Astronomical Clock in the Old Town Square,
       Prague, Czech Republic   168
Church of Our Lady Before Týn, Prague,
Czech Republic   169
View of Buda side of Budapest with
       Buda Castle, Matthias Church and
       Fisherman's Bastion, Budapest, Hungary   170
Vajdahunyad Castle, Budapest, Hungary   171
Heroes' Square, Budapest, Hungary   172
Széchenyi Spa Baths, Budapest, Hungary   174
Parliament Building, Budapest, Hungary   175
Fisherman's Bastion, Budapest, Hungary   176
Statues in Memento Park, Budapest, Hungary   177
St Stephen's Basilica, Budapest, Hungary   178
Széchenyi Chain Bridge, Budapest, Hungary   179
St Charles's Church, Vienna, Austria   180
Johann Strauss in Stadtpark, Vienna, Austria   181
Schönbrunn Palace, Vienna, Austria   182
Belvedere Park, Vienna, Austria   184
Wiener Staatsoper, Vienna, Austria   185
St Stephen's Cathedral, Vienna, Austria   186
Hundertwasser House, Vienna, Austria   187
Museum of Natural History, Vienna, Austria   188

INDEX   **190**

INTRODUCTION

Stretching from exotic Asia in the east to the choppy waves of the Atlantic Ocean in the west and from the sun-kissed shores of the Mediterranean in the south to the frozen wastes of the Arctic in the north, Europe encompasses a vast area of more than 10 million square miles. Around 11 per cent of the world's population lives within its borders but, arguably, a far greater percentage of the world's finest attractions can be found on this continent, from palaces and castles to churches, museums and bridges.

Comedian Eddie Izzard once said 'Europe is where the history comes from' and it is true that probably more of Europe's past has been preserved over the millennia than anywhere else in the world, a continuing story that is illuminated by the great monuments to civilizations, peoples and nations that we visit in our millions every year.

In *Best-Kept Secrets of Europe*, many of these fabulous destinations are sumptuously pictured and their histories and idiosyncrasies explained. The book divides Europe into several useful parts – Western Europe, the Iberian Peninsula, Italy and the Mediterranean, and Eastern and Central Europe, and within those are further sections detailing the principal attractions of 18 of Europe's great destinations, from Dublin to Istanbul and Madrid to Crete, a voyage of discovery that will hopefully make the reader yearn for travel and exploration. And, indeed, Europe's cities reward the adventurous explorer, who will find wonders around the corner of every narrow street and along the length of every spacious boulevard on which he or she is prepared to venture.

In Europe, the traveller is catered for, no matter his or her taste. If it is the forbidding magnificence of castles or fortresses or the glorious splendour of baroque palaces you seek, there are countless suitable destinations across Europe. In this book are stolid citadels such as the castles of Edinburgh, Prague and Rumeli, built for defence and exuding an air of resolute defiance, while the glorious Château de Vincennes,

Charlottenburg Palace and Royal Palace in Madrid show how the other half lived, opening doors on the privileged existence of European royalty in bygone days and elucidating history for the visitor. Of course, the great churches of Europe display another side of the continent, its religious and spiritual life, delineated over the centuries by flying buttresses, towering spires, breathtaking naves and glorious altarpieces. *Best-Kept Secrets of Europe* takes time, however, to cast a glance at some of the continent's quirkier corners, such as the world's oldest surviving restaurant, the Sobrino de Botín in Madrid, and the Scotch Whisky Experience on Edinburgh's Castlehill, a must-see for everyone who loves a dram. Café culture and the modern quest for leisure opportunities are presented in entries for the splendid Mikrolimano Marina in the Greek port of Piraeus or the modern resort of Agios Nikolaos on Crete, for there is nothing in Europe better than making yourself comfortable at a café in a square or by a harbour side and watching the rest of the world stroll past. Piazza San Marco and Campo Santo Stefano in Venice, Trastevere at night, or any café in Paris are ideal for the casual observer of European life in the raw.

Although much of this book is taken up with reminders of Europe's sometimes bloody, sometimes glittering, but always fascinating past, there is time, too, to consider a few of the newer additions to its cities' tourist maps, for example The Samuel Beckett Bridge in Dublin which opened as recently as 2009, and the Bosphorus Bridge which finally spanned the Bosphorus in Istanbul after centuries of debate. If nothing else, the inclusion of these modern attractions reminds us that Europe is still developing and new monuments to progress continue to be built.

Of course, one book is hardly sufficient to uncover the multitude of treasures that Europe has to offer and many more pages could have been filled with what is available to the visitor. Scandinavia is not even covered here but it too has many fascinating attractions. There is one in particular that is not a building, a bridge or a garden. In fact, it takes place in the sky. The Northern Lights – or the *Aurora Borealis* – is a spectacular light show in the heavens that is best viewed from the charming Norwegian town of Tromsø, described in the eighteenth and nineteenth centuries as the 'Paris of the North'. If castles and palaces are your penchant, then Denmark is the place to go. The eighteenth-century Fredensborg Palace, north of Copenhagen, has splendid gardens and Kronborg Castle is one

Old Town, where the city was founded in 1252, is one of the largest and best-preserved medieval city centres in Europe. You feel as if you are in a living museum as you stroll through its narrow, winding cobblestone streets and if you are lucky enough to be there when it snows, you will feel as if you have walked into the pages of a book of fairy tales. The Nobel Museum is located there, dedicated to providing information about the Nobel Prize and Nobel Laureates from 1901 to the present day, and detailing the life of the prestigious award's founder, Alfred Nobel (1833–96).

Finland is a much neglected tourist destination, but there is much to see there. Helsinki, its capital, is a busy city where the country's best museums, galleries, restaurants and shopping can be found. There is marvellous architecture to be savoured, including the 1971 Finlandia Hall, designed by renowned Finnish architect Alvar Aalto, and Senate Square with Helsinki Cathedral, the Government Palace, the University of Helsinki and the National Library of Finland. The underground Temppeliaukio Church – also known as the Rock Church – is hewn out of solid rock and welcomed its first astonished congregation in 1969.

of northern Europe's most important Renaissance castles, not least because William Shakespeare immortalized it as Elsinore in his play *Hamlet*. The Blue Lagoon in Iceland is an example of the geysers to be found in Scandinavia and Reykjavík's warm, relaxing thermal pools are always open, no matter the weather. For the quirkier visit, there is the original Legoland in Billund in Denmark, with 340 million pieces of Lego and numerous exciting rides guaranteed to please children of all ages. Meanwhile, Stockholm, capital of Sweden, has much to offer. The spectacular *Vasa* is the only preserved seventeenth-century ship in the world, painstakingly restored over the last 50 years after being salvaged in 1961. Gamla Stan, Stockholm's

Further east, the states of the Baltic are often visited for stag parties, but even those visitors cannot fail to be impressed by what they see. Tallinn, capital of Estonia, boasts an old town to die for, with medieval architecture, labyrinthine cobblestone streets, iron street lamps and bustling medieval markets. The view from Harju Hill provides a perspective on the old and new of the city and the former harbour area, Andrejsala, once a playground for artists, performers and students nowadays offers a tranquil space to sit and watch the water flow.

What about Poland, a country affected by the tides of European history more than most? Its towns and cities often provide a magical atmosphere and wonderful architecture. Kraków, for instance, the former capital, is one of Europe's most beautiful cities. It has fine examples of Renaissance and baroque architecture in its Wawel Cathedral and the Royal Castle on the banks of the Vistula. Its square is the largest medieval square in Europe and the city is home to Jagiellonian University, founded by Casimir III 'the Great' (1310–70) in 1364, making it one of the oldest universities in the world. Escaping the city, tranquillity can be found and enjoyed in the region of the Masurian Lakes. Tens of thousands of yachtsmen, fishermen, hikers, cyclists and walkers enjoy this peaceful land of around 3,000 lakes that also offers the chance to visit castles in Reszel, Nidzica and Gizycko, the astonishing baroque church in Święta Lipka and Adolf Hitler's (1889–1945) wartime headquarters in the forests near Ketrzyn.

But, even in the countries covered in this book, how many more wonderful places there are to visit! Stonehenge in England, the jostling southern streets of Naples, the beautiful Alhambra in Spain, the Douro River in Portugal, Ireland's rugged west coast, Glasgow's art nouveau treasures, Istanbul's Topkapi Palace, the Theatre at Delphi in Greece, the wonderful Musée d'Orsay in Paris, the Spanish Riding School in Vienna.... The list is endless and indicative of just how fortunate we are to have these treasures available to us to enjoy and to help us to understand the past that has brought us to this point. As Europe uncovers its secrets, so we Europeans uncover the secrets of ourselves. As the great American writer, James Baldwin (1924–87), once said: 'I met a lot of people in Europe. I even encountered myself.'

WESTERN EUROPE

The tides of war and the stain of bloodshed have often blighted the nations of Western Europe, prey to the scourges of ambition and power. But Western Europe is also a region that has produced great thinkers, writers and artists, providing posterity with some of the great movements and people of history.

The Renaissance, the Reformation, the Enlightenment and the Industrial Revolution were all conceived in Western European cities by people born and brought up in its lands, and these brought irrevocable change to the entire world – change that still reverberates today. With that change often came prosperity and we see the results of it in the world around us, in the palaces, castles, churches and cities built by the wealthy and the powerful throughout history and in the museums and galleries that provide an opportunity for all of us to experience great art, such as Leonardo da Vinci's Renaissance masterpiece, the *Mona Lisa* in the Louvre in Paris. Western Europe encompasses the great cities of London, Paris, Dublin, Berlin and many others where great things have been achieved and which we visit in our millions, assimilating the lessons of history or just admiring the beauty and splendour of what is in front of us.

NOTRE DAME

Paris, France

PARC MONTSOURIS

Paris, France

Dominating the Île de la Cité, with its flying buttresses, shimmering rose windows and crouching gargoyles, the beautiful cathedral of Notre Dame is a masterpiece of Gothic architecture. Begun in 1163, during the reign (1137–80) of Louis VII (1120–80), it was completed in 1345. Since then, it has survived invading armies, assaults by Huguenots and revolutionaries and dubious restorations, providing contemplative peace and reflection in the midst of the bustling city. Notre Dame's treasury contains what is claimed to be the Crown of Thorns, a fragment of the True Cross and a Holy Nail.

During his reign from 1852–70, Emperor Napoleon III (1808–73) created four spacious urban public parks in Paris, located at each of the cardinal points of the compass. Joining the Bois de Boulogne in the north, the Bois de Vincennes in the west and the Parc des Buttes in the east was Parc Montsouris, situated in the south of the city. Designed as a beautiful English landscape garden, the park is home to a lake, extensive sloping lawns and a dazzling array of trees, shrubs and flowers.

CHÂTEAU DE VINCENNES

Paris, France

Originally built around 1150 as a hunting lodge for Louis VII, the imposing royal castle, the Château de Vincennes, was substantially enlarged in the thirteenth century, its huge walls being added around 1410. Over the centuries, it has served as a porcelain factory, a prison and an arsenal, and the notorious First World War spy and *femme fatale*, Mata Hari (1876–1917), was executed there. The surrounding park, the Bois de Vincennes, magnificently landscaped in the English style, is the largest public park in Paris.

CAFÉ AT RUE MOUFFETARD

Paris, France

The café is a quintessential part of the Parisian way of life – a convivial place to relax and refuel, to drop in for a quick drink on the way home from work or to enjoy a leisurely lunchtime or evening meal. For centuries, heated discussions about art and politics have exercised minds around wobbly tables that spill out on to pavements often barely wide enough to walk on. Amongst the best-known cafés in Paris are Café de la Paix, Les Deux Magots, Café de Flore and Café de la Rotonde.

THE LOUVRE

Paris, France

Situated on Paris's Rive Gauche, the world's most visited museum, the Louvre, was built as a fortress in the late twelfth century by Philip II (1165–1223). Now more than nine million people visit it annually to view its 35,000 fascinating objects ranging in date from prehistory to the modern day. The Louvre's collection includes many of the world's most famous works of art, including the Venus de Milo (*c.* 130–100 BC) and Leonardo da Vinci's *Mona Lisa* (*c.* 1503–06). Its famous glass and metal pyramid, designed by I.M. Pei (b. 1917), was completed in 1989.

MUSÉE DE L'ORANGERIE

Paris, France

Paris's Musée de l'Orangerie was built in 1852 to provide shelter for the orange trees of the garden of the Tuileries Palace but in the nineteenth century was used as a store, lodgings for soldiers and an event space. In 1921, the Orangerie and the neighbouring building, the Jeu de Paume, became museums and six years later, the Orangerie's redesigned rooms welcomed eight of Impressionist artist Claude Monet's (1840–1926) shimmeringly beautiful *Nymphéas* (Water Lilies) canvases. It now also houses an impressive collection of work by artists such as Cézanne (1839–1906), Picasso (1881–1973), Renoir (1841–1919) and Matisse (1869–1954).

SAINT-SULPICE CHURCH AND FOUNTAIN

Paris, France

Paris's second-largest church after Notre Dame is the late baroque Saint-Sulpice, founded in 1646 on the site of a thirteenth-century Romanesque church and largely completed by 1745, although its south tower remains unfinished. Situated in the Luxembourg quarter on Paris's Rive Gauche, it was the scene of the christenings of the Marquis de Sade (1740–1814), Charles Baudelaire (1821–67) and Victor Hugo (1802–85), amongst others, and is home to frescoes by Eugène Delacroix (1798–1863) and one of the world's largest organs. Fans of *The Da Vinci Code* (2006) will know that Saint-Sulpice plays an important role in Dan Brown's bestseller.

EIFFEL TOWER

Paris, France

Few tourist destinations evoke the spirit of a place as much as the 342 m (1,122 ft) high Eiffel Tower does for Paris. Named after Gustave Eiffel (1832–1923), whose company designed and erected the tower in the Champs de Mars as the entrance arch to the Exposition Universelle of 1889, when it was the tallest edifice ever constructed. It is now the most-visited paid monument in the world, the magnificent panoramic view of Paris that can be enjoyed from the tower's uppermost level attracting almost seven million people a year.

PASSAGE DES PANORAMAS

Paris, France

Between the Boulevard Montmartre to the north and Rue Saint-Marc to the south lies the roofed, shop-lined passageway, the Passage des Panoramas. Built in 1800 and one of the first of its kind in Europe, this ancestor to the city gallerias of the nineteenth century and contemporary shopping malls was initially home to the Paris stamp trade and is described in Émile Zola's (1840–1902) novel, *Nana* (1880). Its name is derived from two rotunda bearing panoramas of a number of cities including Paris, Toulon, Rome and Jerusalem that were an attraction until being destroyed in 1831.

MONTMARTRE

Paris, France

Montmartre is a 130-metre-high hill in Paris's 18th Arondissement from which the surrounding district takes its name. Occupied from at least Gallo-Roman times, the hill is dominated by the gleaming white dome of the Basilica of the Sacré Coeur. In the nineteenth century, the area was famous for its cafés, restaurants, balls and cabarets such as the Chat Noir and the Moulin Rouge, the birthplace of the French Can-Can. Many notable artists lived and worked there, including Pierre Renoir (1841–1919), Claude Monet (1840–1926), Pablo Picasso (1881–1973), Vincent van Gogh (1853–1890) and Salvador Dalí (1904–1989).

PORTOBELLO ROAD

London, England

The energetic, cosmopolitan atmosphere of Portobello Road, in the Notting Hill area of the Royal Borough of Kensington and Chelsea, is created by the range of communities that live along it and the bustling market that hugs its kerbs. Colourful vintage clothing and fruit and vegetable stalls are joined on Saturdays by the United Kingdom's largest antique market and numerous stalls selling bric-a-brac. The stallholders are no less colourful than their wares, and items on offer include glass, crystal, silver, rare books and many other collectibles.

PETER PAN STATUE, KENSINGTON GARDENS

London, England

The Peter Pan statue, located to the west of the section of the Serpentine in Kensington Gardens known as The Long Water, was commissioned by the creator of *Peter Pan*, the Scottish author and dramatist, J.M. Barrie (1860–1937). Sculpted by Sir George Frampton (1860–1928), the statue was erected in 1912 at the exact spot on which Peter Pan lands after flying out of the Darling family nursery. It features an array of squirrels, rabbits, mice and fairies climbing up to Peter at the top of the bronze statue.

ST PAUL'S CATHEDRAL

London, England

The Anglican cathedral of St Paul's, dominated by its world-famous dome, is an iconic feature of the London skyline and a cathedral dedicated to St Paul has stood on this site, the highest point in the City of London, for more than 1,400 years. The present building is the masterpiece of Britain's most famous architect, Sir Christopher Wren (1632–1723), designed in the baroque style, and built between 1675 and 1720. It became a symbol of Britain's steadfastness during the Second World War when it stood untouched amidst the smoke and fire of the Blitz.

KEW GARDENS

London, England

Founded in 1840, Kew Gardens is one of the oldest and most popular botanical gardens in the world, with between one and two million people visiting annually. It is host to 30,000 different types of plants, the world's largest collection of living plants, and its herbarium contains a staggering seven million preserved plant specimens. It consists of 121 ha (299 ac) of gardens and botanical glasshouses, some of which are listed, all set in an internationally significant landscape. In 2003, it was added to UNESCO's list of World Heritage Sites.

TOWER BRIDGE

London, England

Like the Eiffel Tower in Paris, the splendidly majestic Tower Bridge is emblematic of the city in which it stands, its twin towers rising over the Thames, holding up the suspended sections of the bridge on which runs a road linking the south and north of the city. Begun in 1886 and opened in 1894, it was built in response to increased commercial development in London's East End, employing a drawbridge design that allowed tall-masted ships to access port facilities in the Pool of London between the Tower of London and London Bridge.

LEADENHALL MARKET

London, England

Leadenhall Market may be strangely familiar to many people, having featured in the film *Harry Potter and the Philosopher's Stone* (2001), in which it represented the fictional area of London near The Leaky Cauldron and Diagon Alley. This covered market in the City of London is on the site of one of the oldest markets in London, dating back to the fourteenth century, with its magnificently ornate maroon, cream and green roof structure and cobbled floors designed in 1881 by Sir Horace Jones (1819–87). It was originally a market for meat, game and poultry, but is now home to a variety of retailers, restaurants and bars. In the 2012 Olympics, it formed part of the marathon course.

THE SHERLOCK HOLMES MUSEUM

London, England

The privately run Sherlock Holmes Museum is located at 221B Baker Street, said to be the world's most famous address. It was here that the famous fictional detective of Sir Arthur Conan Doyle's (1859–1930) hugely popular books is supposed to have lived from 1881 to 1904 with his friend and assistant, Dr Watson, as tenants of the fussy Mrs Hudson. Although the doorway sits between numbers 237 and 241, the Sherlock Holmes Society of England has been given special permission by the City of Westminster to use the number 221B.

THE ITALIAN GARDENS, KENSINGTON GARDENS

London, England

On the north side of Kensington Gardens near Lancaster Gate lies the 155-year-old water garden known as the Italian Gardens. Created in 1860 as a gift from Prince Albert (1819–61) to his beloved wife, Queen Victoria (1819–1901), the garden, designed by James Pennethorne (1801–71), is based on the gardens at Osborne House on the Isle of Wight. It comprises four main basins with central rosettes, all elaborately carved in Carrara marble, and the famous Portland stone and white marble Tazza Fountain that overlooks The Long Water.

NATIONAL MARITIME MUSEUM, GREENWICH

London, England

Seen here against the backdrop of Canary Wharf, the National Maritime Museum is the largest of its kind in the world. Its historic buildings form part of the Maritime Greenwich World Heritage Site and include the Royal Observatory, the location of the Prime Meridian; the Cutty Sark, the last surviving tea clipper; and the Queen's House, the seventeenth-century former royal residence designed by Inigo Jones (1573–1652). The museum helps to provide visitors with an understanding of Britain's economic, social, political and maritime history and the impact it has had on the world in which we live.

BIG BEN AND THE
HOUSES OF PARLIAMENT

London, England

The Palace of Westminster is where the British House
of Commons and House of Lords meet. Often known as
the Houses of Parliament, it lies on the north bank of
the River Thames, built to replace a medieval complex
destroyed by fire in 1834. The new palace was designed
in the Perpendicular Gothic style by Sir Charles Barry
(1795–1860), who was assisted by Gothic architecture expert
Augustus Pugin (1812–52). The Elizabeth Tower, at the
palace's north end, houses the great bell, known as Big Ben,
whose name is often extended to the bell tower itself.

SCOTT MONUMENT

Edinburgh, Scotland

Scottish author Sir Walter Scott (1771–1832) – writer of novels such as *Waverley* (1814) and *Ivanhoe* (1820) – was the first English-language author to enjoy a truly international career in his lifetime. Following his death, a competition was held to find the best design for a monument to him. George Meikle Kemp's (1795–1844) winning Victorian Gothic design features 64 characters from Scott's novels and a statue of the author fashioned from white Italian marble by Scottish sculptor John Steel (1804–91). Completed in 1844, it is the largest monument to a writer in the world.

ST GILES CATHEDRAL

Edinburgh, Scotland

With its distinctive crown spire, St Giles Cathedral is the High Kirk of Edinburgh and the Mother Church of Presbyterianism. Situated on the Royal Mile that runs from Holyrood Palace to Edinburgh Castle, the church has been one of Edinburgh's religious focal points for around 900 years. The present building dates from the late fourteenth century, although it was extensively restored in the nineteenth century. It contains the Thistle Chapel, the chapel of Scotland's foremost order of chivalry, The Most Ancient and Most Noble Order of the Thistle.

ARTHUR'S SEAT AND EDINBURGH CITYSCAPE

Edinburgh, Scotland

Rising to a height of 251 m (824 ft) above Edinburgh, the hill known as Arthur's Seat rewards the viewer with a spectacular panorama of the city. It is the main peak of a group of hills that make up most of Holyrood Park, created in 1541 by King James V about 1.6 km (1 m) from Edinburgh Castle. In this view over the city, the stronghold of Edinburgh Castle can be seen perched on Castle Rock. To the right is the spire of the Scott Monument and the Firth of Forth flows in the background.

THE SCOTCH WHISKY EXPERIENCE

Edinburgh, Scotland

Scotland's national drink has been distilled since at least the late 1400s and is now enjoyed all over the world. The Scotch Whisky Experience, on Castlehill in Edinburgh's historic Old Town, offers the ultimate tour of the world of whisky with an exhilarating whisky barrel ride around a virtual distillery and a guided tasting in which all the different flavours and styles of 'the water of life' can be savoured. The building is home to the 3,384 bottles of the Diageo Claive Vidiz Whisky Collection, the world's largest collection of whiskies.

EDINBURGH CASTLE

Edinburgh, Scotland

Castle Rock, on which the impressive historic fortress of Edinburgh Castle stands, has been occupied by humans since at least the Iron Age and there has been a royal castle there since at least the reign of David I (1084–1153), King of the Scots from 1124 to his death. Involved in many historic conflicts over the centuries, from the fourteenth-century Wars of Scottish Independence to the Jacobite Rising of 1745 that sought to put Bonnie Prince Charlie (1720–88) on the British throne, it has been a military barracks since the seventeenth century.

DEAN GALLERY

Edinburgh, Scotland

Originally designed as an orphanage in 1831 by the Scottish Greek Revivalist architect Thomas Hamilton (1784–1858), Dean Gallery was for many decades an education centre and since 1999 has been part of the National Galleries of Scotland. Located opposite its sister gallery, the Scottish National Gallery of Modern Art, it houses the Paolozzi Gift, a collection of works donated by Scottish artist Sir Eduardo Paolozzi (1924–2005), and a large collection of Dada and Surrealist art and literature. Behind it lies the Dean Cemetery, its grandiose monuments providing a rich source of Edinburgh and Victorian history.

LEITH HARBOUR

Edinburgh, Scotland

Situated on the coast of the Firth of Forth, Leith has been a port since the twelfth century and, as the port of Scotland's capital, has been the site of many significant historical events. After the Second World War, the docks at Leith went into serious decline, but in recent years, the area has undergone

considerable regeneration and is now a bustling harbour visited by luxurious cruise liners. It is home to the decommissioned Royal Yacht Britannia, which is permanently berthed at Ocean Terminal, the magnificent shopping centre designed by Sir Terence Conran (b. 1931).

WELLINGTON MONUMENT, PHOENIX PARK

Dublin, Ireland

The Phoenix Park monument to the British General Arthur Wellesley, 1st Duke of Wellington (1769–1852), is the tallest obelisk in Europe, standing at 62 m (203 ft). Erected to commemorate the achievements of the Dublin-born victor of Waterloo, it stands in the south-east end of the park, overlooking the Dublin suburb of Kilmainham and the River Liffey. The memorial was originally planned for Merrion Square in Dublin, but was relocated after objections by residents. Designed in 1817 by the architect Sir Robert Smirke (1780–1867), the project ran out of funds in 1820 and was not completed until 1861.

LAKE AT FARMLEIGH

Dublin, Ireland

Formerly one of the residences of the Guinness family, the eighteenth-century Georgian house, Farmleigh, in Phoenix Park, Dublin, is now the official Irish State guesthouse. It has welcomed many distinguished visitors, including prime ministers, presidents, kings and queens, and Queen Elizabeth II and the Duke of Edinburgh spent three nights there during their state visit to the Republic in 2011. This beautiful estate boasts extensive gardens, including a walled garden and a sunken garden, as well as a boating pond and a herd of rare, native Kerry cattle.

TEMPLE BAR

Dublin, Ireland

On the south bank of the River Liffey in the centre of Dublin
lies the culturally vibrant quarter known as Temple Bar, with
its lively nightlife and famous pubs such as the Palace Bar, the
Temple Bar and the Oliver St John Gogarty. From the eighteenth
to the late twentieth centuries, it was blighted by urban decay, but
was revived in the 1980s when small shops, artists and galleries
began to be attracted to the area. It is now home to many Irish
cultural institutions, but it is at night that it comes alive.

PLATO SCULPTURE, TRINITY COLLEGE LIBRARY

Dublin, Ireland

The library of Trinity College and the University of Dublin is the
largest library in Ireland and home to Ireland's greatest national
treasure – the illuminated manuscript Gospel book, the *Book of
Kells*, thought to have been written and illustrated around 800.
The *Book of Kells* was donated to the library in 1661, but the
library first opened with the founding of Trinity College in 1592.
The main chamber of the library, built between 1712 and 1732,
is lined with marble busts and houses 200,000 of its oldest books.

THE SAMUEL BECKETT BRIDGE

Dublin, Ireland

The Samuel Beckett Bridge, joining Sir John Rogerson's Quay on the south of the River Liffey and Guild Street and North Wall Quay in the Docklands area of Dublin, was officially opened in December 2009. Designed by the Spanish Neo-Futurist architect, Santiago Calatrava (b. 1951), it commemorates the life of the Irish avant-garde playwright, novelist, theatre director and poet, Samuel Beckett (1906–89), writer of plays such as *Waiting for Godot* (1953), *Happy Days* (1961) and *Not I* (1972). The design is said to evoke the shape of Ireland's national symbol, the harp, lying on its edge.

CHRIST CHURCH CATHEDRAL

Dublin, Ireland

Located in the heart of what was once medieval Dublin, Christ Church was probably founded sometime around 1030, following a pilgrimage to Rome by the Hiberno-Norse King of Dublin, Sitric Silkenbeard (*c.* 970–1042). Its decaying structure was heavily renovated in the 1870s, but it remains a fascinating mixture of the surviving medieval elements and nineteenth-century church building. The addition of seven bells to the cathedral in 1999 took the number to 19, a world record for the number of church bells. It also has the largest cathedral crypt in Britain or Ireland at 63.4 m (208 ft) long.

STEPHEN'S GREEN SHOPPING CENTRE

Dublin, Ireland

At the top of Dublin's busiest thoroughfare, Grafton Street, in the south side of Dublin City, is Stephen's Green Shopping Centre. The site includes the area where once stood the Dandelion Market where U2 played several of their earliest gigs and where, until 1981, stalls sold punk paraphernalia and clothes. The shopping centre takes its name from the nearby park, St Stephen's Green, which was opened to the public in 1880 and includes a garden for the blind with scented flowers that can withstand handling and which are labelled in Braille.

BERLIN CATHEDRAL

Berlin, Germany

The impressively domed Berlin Cathedral had its beginnings in 1451 when Prince-Elector Frederick 'Irontooth' of Brandenburg (1413–71) returned from Jerusalem via Rome and elevated the chapel in his City Palace in Berlin to a parish church. The largest church in the city, major rebuilding was begun in 1894, but after suffering substantial damage during the Second World War, it took until 1975 to begin its reconstruction. The work was finally completed in 1993. The top of the dome rewards those brave enough to make the climb with a stunning view of Berlin.

THE CUPOLA ON TOP OF THE REICHSTAG BUILDING

Berlin, Germany

The Reichstag Building in Berlin was constructed to house the Imperial Diet or Parliament of the German Empire in 1894. Severely damaged by fire in 1933, it fell into disuse and it was only after German Reunification in October 1990 that reconstruction, led by British architect Sir Norman Foster (b. 1935), began. The spectacular large glass dome at the very top of the Reichstag offers a 360-degree view of the surrounding cityscape and spills natural light down to the floor of the parliament that now once again sits in the building.

HAUS DER KULTUREN DER WELT

Berlin, Germany

The Haus der Kulturen der Welt is situated in Berlin's Tiergarten Park. Formerly a conference venue donated to Germany by the United States, its roof collapsed in 1880 and in 1987, it was rebuilt in its original style in time for the 750th anniversary of the founding of the city of Berlin. It is now Germany's national centre for international contemporary arts, hosting exhibitions, films, performances and conferences. In the middle of a circular basin at the entrance stands British sculptor Henry Moore's (1898–1986) final major work, *Large Divided Oval: Butterfly* (1985–86).

TIERGARTEN

Berlin, Germany

Dating back to 1527, the Tiergarten is the oldest public park in Berlin. Founded as an area in which the Electors of Brandenburg could hunt, it was badly damaged during the Second World War and it was not until 1955 that restoration began. Now, there is much to see in its 2.5 sq km (1 sq m) of parkland. The Victory Column commemorates victory in the Prusso-Danish War of 1864, while nearby is the Bellevue Palace, residence of the German President, and a monument celebrating the achievements of the composers Beethoven (1712–73), Haydn (1732–1809) and Mozart (1756–91).

CHARLOTTENBURG PALACE

Berlin, Germany

Built at the end of the seventeenth century and added to during the eighteenth century, the Charlottenburg Palace is the largest palace in Berlin and the only one dating back to the time of the Hohenzollern family who were electors of Brandenburg, kings of Prussia and emperors of Germany. The palace's interior is elegantly decorated in the baroque and rococo styles and it is surrounded by a large formal garden and woodland that includes a belvedere, a mausoleum, a theatre and a pavilion. Damaged in the Second World War, it has been extensively restored.

BERLIN WALL

Berlin, Germany

One of the most trenchant symbols of the Cold War that blighted relations between east and west after the war, the Berlin Wall divided the city of Berlin between 1961 and 1989. It included guard towers situated at intervals along its concrete walls and between east and west was the death strip where more than 200 people are estimated to have been killed trying to make the crossing. The 1989 collapse of the Eastern Bloc led to great celebrations, the demolition of the wall and the reunification of Germany.

THE OBERBAUM BRIDGE

Berlin, Germany

The remarkable Oberbaum Bridge, crossing the River Spree, links Friedrichshain and Kreuzberg. These two places were once divided by the Berlin Wall and the bridge, therefore, has come to represent an important symbol of the city's unity. Designed in the north German Brick Gothic style, it is a double-deck bridge, the lower deck carrying a road and the upper deck carrying the Berlin U-Bahn – or underground railway – and, with its magnificent twin towers, resembles a city gate with decorative elements such as coats of arms, pointed arches and cross vaults.

RIJKSMUSEUM

Amsterdam, The Netherlands

Founded in The Hague in 1800 and relocated to Amsterdam in 1808, the Rijksmuseum is the national museum of the Netherlands, dedicated to art and history. Within its walls can be viewed around 8,000 objects from the total collection of around one million dating from 1200 to the present day, amongst which can be found masterpieces such as *The Night Watch* (1642) by Rembrandt (1606–69), as well as work by other Dutch masters such as Frans Hals (*c.* 1580–1666), Johannes Vermeer (1632–75) and Vincent van Gogh (1853–90). The museum has recently undergone a dazzling €375 million refurbishment.

TULIPS, AMSTERDAM FLOWER MARKET

Amsterdam, The Netherlands

The tulip is an enduring Dutch symbol, first grown by the sixteenth century's most influential horticulturalist, Carolus Clusius (1526–1609) in Leiden in the Netherlands in 1594. Bizarrely, between 1634 and 1637, the enthusiasm for the new flowers triggered a speculative frenzy in the Netherlands known as the 'tulip mania', when tulip bulbs became so expensive that they were treated as a form of currency. The market collapsed in 1637, but at its height, some single tulip bulbs sold for more than 10 times the annual income of a skilled craftsman.

ANNE FRANK STATUE, NEAR THE ANNE FRANK MUSEUM

Amsterdam, The Netherlands

Anne Frank (1929–1945) was a Jewish girl who, following the Nazi occupation of the Netherlands, was forced with her family into hiding in 1942 in rooms in the building where her father worked. After two years, the Frank family was betrayed and transported to concentration camps, where, like millions of others, all but Anne's father, Otto Frank (1889–1980), perished. Following the war, Anne gained posthumous international fame when the diary she had kept while in hiding, *The Diary of a Young Girl* (1947), became a bestseller. This charming statue of a smiling Anne is located near the Anne Frank Museum.

THE MODERN EYE FILM INSTITUTE BY THE IJ HARBOUR

Amsterdam, The Netherlands

On a bend in the River IJ, opposite the historic part of Amsterdam and its Central Station, sits the spectacular modern building that houses the EYE Film Institute. The architects have employed the concept of film as an illusion of light, space and movement made real through projection to create a gleaming white building with multiple layers, etched with countless interlaced, trapezoidal forms. The IJ waterfront has been transformed in recent years and is now home to apartment blocks, offices, businesses and cultural institutions.

SINGEL CANAL

Amsterdam, The Netherlands

The Singel Canal functioned as a moat around Amsterdam until 1585 when the city began to expand. It is now the innermost canal in the semicircular ring of canals that flow through the city. The famous floating Amsterdam flower market, the Bloemenmarkt, the market stalls of which are actually boats, can be found on the banks of the Singel, and it is also home to a designated red-light district, Singelgebied. The canal is lined by many beautiful, extravagantly decorated canal houses built during the Dutch Golden Age.

THE IBERIAN PENINSULA

Barcelona, Madrid and Lisbon are the Iberian Peninsula's three great cities, each with its own peculiar and fascinating history.

The seaside city of Barcelona, for instance, wears its Catalonian heritage with pride, but it is also one of Europe's top destinations, and deservedly so, with its world-class dining, Gothic Quarter and uniquely individual architecture, courtesy of the Modernist architect Antoni Gaudí. Its more serious Spanish cousin, Madrid, is a little more reserved; understandably, as the capital is home to Spain's great institutions such as the royal family, the government and the magnificent Golden Triangle of Art that takes in the Museo del Prado, the Reina Sofía Museum and the Museo Thyssen-Bornemisza. One might be tempted to think Barcelona has all the fun, but in reality, Madrid is just as exciting a city to visit with magnificent architecture, great art and fine dining aplenty. Across the border in Portugal, Lisbon is a grand old city, capital of a country that helped shape the modern world during the Age of Discovery that began in the early fifteenth century and culminated in the discovery by Vasco da Gama (*c.* 1460s–1524), sailing under a Portuguese flag, of a trade route to India. That golden age is ever-present in the many attractions that Lisbon offers the visitor.

GAUDI'S CASA BATLLÓ

Barcelona, Spain

The unique genius of the architect, Antoni Gaudí (1852–1926), has come to define Barcelona's aesthetic. His instantly recognizable style is expressive and individualistic, part Modernism, part neo-Gothic, but with elements of cubism and surrealism, and creates a vibrant, colourful reflection of the Catalan soul. With its multi-coloured roof tiles, balconies that resemble skulls and window supports that resemble bones, Casa Batlló is a fine example of his unique vision. His remarkable masterpiece, the Sagrada Familia church is on course to finally be completed in 2026, building having begun in 1882.

PARC DEL LABERINT D'HORTA

Barcelona, Spain

Far from the normal tourist routes is the peace and quiet of the Parc del Laberint d'Horta, the oldest park in Barcelona, which was built in the late eighteenth century by the Marquis Desvall for the Catalan nobility. Made up of an eighteenth-century neoclassical garden and a nineteenth-century romantic garden, the park contains a labyrinth created in 1792, made up of about 750 m (about 2,460 ft) of precisely trimmed cypress hedge. In the centre of the labyrinth is a statue of the huntress Diana armed with a bow.

BARCELONA BEACH

Barcelona, Spain

Not many major cities have beaches on their doorsteps on which the population and tourists alike can take their ease in the sun. Barcelona has several, one of which, La Barceloneta, in the Ciutat Vella district, is actually mentioned in Cervantes' (1547–1616) *Don Quixote* (two volumes: 1605 and 1615). As sun-worshippers soak up the rays, they may wish to feast their eyes on German artist Rebecca Horn's (b. 1944) *Homenatge a la Barceloneta* structure (2013), a leaning tower of steel boxes. Meanwhile, along the beach stands a sculpture by renowned American architect, Frank Gehry (b. 1929), a giant goldfish named *Peix d'Or* (1992).

LA BOQUERIA MARKET

Barcelona, Spain

Situated on the bustling La Rambla, Barcelona's most famous
street, the Mercat de Sant Josep de la Boqueria assaults the
senses with an explosion of colours, smells and tastes. La
Boqueria has been in existence since at least 1217, when
market stalls selling meat were set up near the gate to the city.
Merchants now vie with each other to create the most attractive
displays of goods which include a huge selection of sweets,
honey, cheese, refined oils, olives, local and exotic fruit and
vegetables, meat, ham, fish and exquisite seafood.

RESTAURANTS AT PLAÇA REIAL

Barcelona, Spain

The palm trees of Plaça Reial and the umbrellas of its many
wonderful restaurants lend it a truly Mediterranean air. Located
in Barcelona's Barri Gòtic – or Gothic Quarter – the centre of
the old city of Barcelona, it lies next to La Rambla and boasts
lanterns designed by Catalonian architect Antoni Gaudí. It is a
popular tourist destination, especially at night when the
restaurants that line its edges are busy with diners. There are
many outdoor events in the square, including open-air concerts,
and it is a popular meeting place for locals and tourists.

PARC GÜELL

Barcelona, Spain

The world-famous Parc Güell is one of Barcelona's greatest attractions. Composed of exotic gardens and fabulous buildings, it was conceived by Catalan entrepreneur Eusebi Güell (1846–1918) and designed by Barcelona's most famous son, the architect Antoni Gaudí. Building of the park took place between 1900 and 1914 and it officially opened to the public in 1926. Gaudí's vision was inspired by organic shapes found in nature, and the park contains a maze of trails, colourfully tiled walls and bridges. In 1984, it was named a UNESCO World Heritage Site.

CARRER DEL BISBE, GOTHIC QUARTER

Barcelona, Spain

Stretching from La Rambla to Via Laietana and from the city's
Mediterranean seafront to Ronda de Sant Pere, the Gothic Quarter,
with its atmospheric medieval buildings, narrow, labyrinthine
thoroughfares and quiet churches, represents the old city of
Barcelona. Remains of the city's Roman wall can be seen and it is
also home to El Call, the medieval Jewish Quarter. Amongst the
area's attractions are the magnificent Barcelona Cathedral and the
Museu Picasso which houses one of the world's most extensive
collections of work by one of the twentieth century's greatest artists.

ARC DE TRIOMF

Barcelona, Spain

The monumental Arc de Triomf – or Triumphal Arch – was
constructed as the main gate for the 1888 Barcelona Universal
Exposition. It was designed by the Catalan architect Josep Vilaseca
i Casanovas (1848–1910), who was a follower of the Modernist
Movement. Constructed of reddish brickwork, it is in the *Neo-
Mudéjar* – or Moorish Revival – style, and bears friezes, one of
which says 'Barcelona rep les nacions' (Catalan for 'Barcelona
welcomes the nations'). The arch stands on Passeig de Luis
Companys, a wide promenade leading to Parc de la Ciutadella.

THE CENTRE OF BARCELONA

Barcelona, Spain

Barcelona provides a unique blend of Catalan culture, distinctive architecture, lively nightlife, cutting-edge and traditional restaurants, as well as bars and stylish hotels. There is also Europe's best-preserved Gothic Quarter and the astonishingly beautiful architectural achievements of Antoni Gaudí, including his unfinished masterpiece, the staggering La Sagrada Familia. At every corner, there is something to see, from wide, elegant boulevards to dimly lit, narrow streets lined with fascinating buildings and eighteenth-century parks to Modernist playgrounds. It is one of the world's truly great cities.

MUSEU NACIONAL D'ART DE CATALUNYA

Barcelona, Spain

Barcelona's National Palace of Montjuïc, known as Palau Nacional, with its dome modelled on St Peter's Basilica in Rome, was completed in 1929 with an interior decorated by many of the most outstanding painters and sculptors of the time. Home to the Museu Nacional d'Art de Catalunya, the museum is known for its outstanding collection of Romanesque church paintings and Catalan art and design of the late nineteenth and early twentieth centuries. Amongst its Romanesque collection are many priceless works that originally adorned rural churches in the Pyrenees and other Catalan sites.

GAUDÍ CHIMNEY AT CASA MILÀ

Barcelona, Spain

More popularly known as La Pedrera, meaning 'The Quarry', the Modernist masterpiece Casa Milà was the last civil work that Antoni Gaudí designed. Built between 1906 and 1910, it was commissioned by the businessman Pere Milà i Camps (1874–1940) and his wife Roser Segimon i Artells (1870–1964). It was a highly innovative construction, having a self-supporting stone front, and columns and floors that were free of load-bearing walls. Even more innovative was its underground garage! The devout Gaudí envisioned the house as spiritually symbolic and introduced many religious elements into his design.

SOBRINO DE BOTÍN RESTAURANT

Madrid, Spain

The great American author Ernest Hemingway (1899–1961) was a regular diner at Sobrino and rated it so highly that it got a mention, along with its signature dish, *cochinillo asado* (roast suckling pig), in his novel *The Sun Also Rises* (1926). The oldest restaurant still running in the world, Sobrino was founded in 1725 by a Frenchman, Jean Botín, and adopted its current name (meaning 'Nephew of Botín') when it was inherited by his nephew. It is said that the great Spanish Romantic painter Goya worked as a dishwasher in the restaurant's kitchen.

CIBELES FOUNTAIN

Madrid, Spain

The striking neoclassical complex of marble sculptures and fountains that sits in Madrid's Plaza de Cibeles has become an important symbol of the city of Madrid. The Cibeles Fountain depicts the Phrygian goddess, Cybele, seated on a chariot that is pulled by two lions. It was built between 1777 and 1782, during the reign of Spanish King Charles III (1716–88), having been designed by the Madrid architect and artist Ventura Rodríguez (1717–85). Fans of the football club Real Madrid flood the square when their team wins and Cybele is often wrapped in a Real Madrid flag.

REINA SOFIA MUSEUM

Madrid, Spain

'El Reina Sofia' or 'the Sofia', as it is popularly known, is Spain's national museum of twentieth-century art, inaugurated in 1992 and named for the wife of the former King Juan Carlos I (b. 1938). It makes up one corner of Madrid's so-called Golden Triangle of Art that also includes the Museo del Prado and the Museo Thyssen-Bornemisza. Mainly dedicated to Spanish art, the Sofia has superb collections of the work of two of Spain's greatest twentieth-century masters: Salvador Dalí (1904–89) and Pablo Picasso (1881–1973), including Picasso's world-famous *Guernica* of 1937.

CRYSTAL PALACE IN RETIRO PARK

Madrid, Spain

Madrid's Buen Retiro Park is home to the imposing glass structure, the Palacio de Cristal – or Crystal Palace – which was built in 1887 to house flora and fauna that were part of an exhibition dedicated to the Philippines, at the time a Spanish colony. Designed by the respected architect, Ricardo Velázquez Bosco (1843–1923), the building is laid out in the shape of a Greek cross made entirely of glass, set in an iron framework that is rooted in a brick base. It is used now for contemporary art exhibitions.

THE ROYAL PALACE

Madrid, Spain

The Palacio Real is Madrid's largest building and arguably
its most beautiful. It is, in fact, the largest royal palace in
Western Europe, occupying a site that once housed the
Alcázar, the Moorish castle that was destroyed by fire in
1734. Originally designed by Filippo Juvara for Felipe V's
court of more than 3,000 courtiers, it was begun in 1738
and completed in 1755. The palace covers 135,000 sq m
(1,453,128 sq ft), has 3,418 rooms and on its walls hang
paintings by Caravaggio (1571–1610), Velázquez, Tiepolo
(1696–1770) and Goya (1746–1828), amongst others.

ROSSIO SQUARE, BAIXA DISTRICT

Lisbon, Portugal

At the heart of the city of Lisbon is the Pedro IV Square, popularly known as Rossio Square, where people take time to sit and relax and perhaps enjoy a drink in one of its atmospheric cafés. Paved with cobblestones in wave patterns, this nineteenth-century square features two magnificent baroque fountains and in the centre is a monument to King Dom Pedro IV (1798–1834), whose statue stands 27 m (89 ft) above the activity below. On the north side stands the Dona Maria II National Theatre, a monumental neoclassical building constructed in the 1840s.

HISTORICAL HOUSE IN ALFAMA

Lisbon, Portugal

A visit to the Alfama, Lisbon's oldest district, with its atmospheric, narrow, winding streets and steep stairs, is to take a step back in time to experience the sights, sounds and smells of the old city. It is redolent of the two cultures that created the city – Roman and Arab – and there are remains of each to be viewed. Situated on the slope between the São Jorge Castle and the River Tagus, the Alfama contains numerous fascinating historic attractions and boasts an abundance of lively Fado bars and restaurants.

TRAMS ON BICA FUNICULAR, NEAR BAIRRO ALTO

Lisbon, Portugal

Since 1892, the Elevador da Bica has provided one of Lisbon's unique modes of transport, a funicular railway transporting passengers 245 m (804 ft) up the dramatically steep Rua da Bica de Duarte Belo from Rua S. Paulo to a panoramic view at the top. It is situated in the charming quarter of Bica where, due to the steepness of its narrow streets and its densely packed buildings, there are few cars to disturb the peace. Designed by Raoul Mesnier de Ponsard (1849–1914), it was designated a national monument in 2002.

QUELUZ NATIONAL PALACE

Lisbon, Portugal

One of Portugal's finest examples of rococo architecture, the Queluz Palace was first built in the seventeenth century as a manor house for King Pedro II (1648–1706), but has since been enlarged and transformed into a beautiful palace. Inside can be viewed the grandiose but elegant Throne Room that would once have resounded to the sound of balls and banquets, the Music Room where concerts and operas were once performed, and the royal bedroom with its stunning murals depicting the adventures of Cervantes' Don Quixote. The palace now provides luxurious accommodation for state guests and dignitaries.

JERÓNIMOS MONASTERY

Lisbon, Portugal

Nowhere is the power and wealth of Portugal during the
Age of Discovery more evident than in the impressive
Jerónimos Monastery, built in 1502 by King Manuel I
(1469–1521) on the site of a hermitage where Vasco da
Gama and his crew spent their last night before embarking
on the voyage in which they discovered the sea route to
India. The great explorer's tomb lies inside the entrance
to the monastery, whose columns are carved with coils
of rope, sea monsters, coral and other maritime motifs in
commemoration of the astonishing achievements of the time.

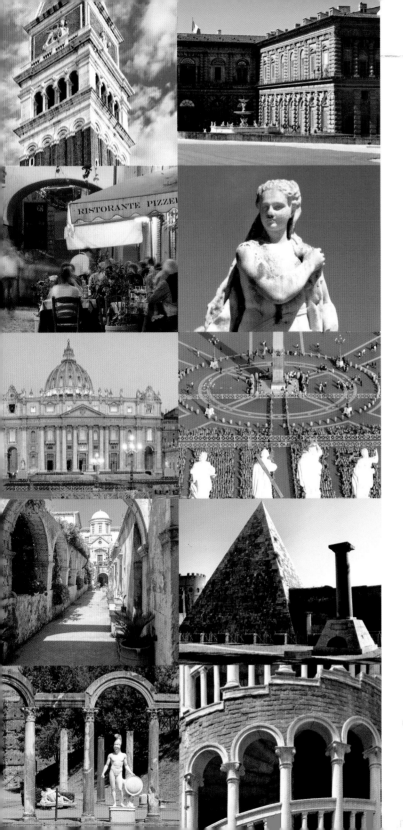

ITALY AND THE MEDITERRANEAN

The south of Europe from Italy through Greece and Crete to Turkey encompasses some of the continent's greatest historical periods and some of the greatest achievements of humankind.

These are lands of great ancient civilizations in which the beginnings of Western thought and culture occurred, and of great and powerful men and families. Traces of the Ancient Greeks, the Roman Empire and the Minoan civilization of Crete can be found in the following pages, their astonishing achievements evident in what they left behind for future generations to marvel at and try to aspire to. But in Venice and Florence, too, great men and great families achieved great things. The influence of the Medici family on the history and fabric of Italy cannot be overestimated, for instance. Their extraordinary wealth and power enabled the building of the Uffizi Gallery and the Palazzo Pitti, now two of the world's finest museums. Wealth and power were also at the root of some of Istanbul's greatest buildings. In this city, teetering on the very edge of Europe, are some of the continent's most astonishing buildings, engineering marvels of their time, built by men of great vision and spirituality.

COLOSSEUM

Rome, Italy

Possibly the most thrilling of all the splendid sights of Rome
is the great gladiatorial arena, the Colosseum. Completed in
AD 80 for the Emperor Vespasian (AD 9–79), it hosted
spectacular gladiatorial contests in front of huge crowds of
bloodthirsty Romans. Games lasted a hundred days and nights
and during that time about 5,000 animals were slaughtered. There
are three levels of arches and at the top, a canvas awning would
have provided shelter for spectators. The arena was abandoned
with the fall of the Roman Empire in the sixth century.

STREET IN TRASTEVERE

Rome, Italy

At night, the narrow, cobbled streets of Trastevere bustle with
tourists, flocking to its bars and restaurants and sampling the heady
nightlife and original character of this ancient part of Rome. The
city's favourite neighbourhood lies across the River Tiber from
many of Rome's main attractions, a former working-class district
that oozes medieval charm and has a little bit of an edge. Trastevere
also has many attractions, including the Palazzo Corsini with
paintings by Titian (c. 1490–1576) and Caravaggio, while Raphael's
frescoes illuminate the walls of the opulent Villa Farnesina.

ANCIENT ROMAN RUINS OF A BAKERY, OSTIA ANTICA

Rome, Italy

Away from the bustle of central Rome lies Ostia Antica, one of Lazio's most popular attractions. Founded in the fourth century BC, Ostia was once Rome's main seaport and with a population of 50,000 was an important defensive and commercial centre. The city went into decline in the fifth century AD as a result of barbarian invasions and finally an outbreak of malaria led to its abandonment and its centuries-long burial in river silt. Its ruins remain tantalizingly intact and a delight to explore.

HADRIAN'S VILLA

Rome, Italy

The Villa Adriana, at Tivoli, just 36 km (22 m) from Rome, is an exceptional complex of classical buildings constructed in the second century AD by the Roman emperor, Hadrian (76–138). This stunning architectural masterpiece brings together the best of the architectural cultures of the ancient Mediterranean world – Egyptian, Greek and Roman – to create the 'ideal city'. The imperial residence was built between 118–38 but after Hadrian's death, his successors added to the complex. Amongst the best-preserved ruins are a pool and an artificial grotto named Canopus and Serapeum, respectively.

ST PETER'S SQUARE

Rome, Italy

One of the holiest sites of the Roman Catholic Church, St Peter's Square was designed by Gian Lorenzo Bernini (1598–1680) and laid out between 1656 and 1667 during the papacy (1655–67) of Alexander VII (1599–1667). From above, the square takes the shape of a giant keyhole with two semicircular colonnades – described by Bernini as 'the motherly arms of the church' – that funnel believers into St Peter's Basilica. In the centre of the square is an obelisk brought from Egypt by Roman Emperor Caligula (AD 12–41) and used by Emperor Nero (AD 37–68) as a turning point in chariot races.

TREVI FOUNTAIN

Rome, Italy

Rome's most famous fountain achieved iconic status when
beautiful Swedish actress Anita Ekberg (1931–2015) went for
a paddle in it in Frederico Fellini's (1920–93) 1960 celluloid
masterpiece, *La Dolce Vita*. This splendidly exuberant baroque
masterpiece, designed by Nicola Salvi (1697–1751) in 1732,
depicts Neptune's chariot being led by Tritons with sea horses,
one of which is wild, the other tame, representing the moods of
the sea. The fountain's name derives from the 'tre vie' – three
roads – that converge there. Superstition dictates that throwing
a coin into the water will ensure a return to the Eternal City.

THE SPANISH STEPS

Rome, Italy

The Spanish Steps teem daily with tourists of every nationality
who sit and relax, watching the world go by or snapping countless
photographs. Climbing the steep slope from the Piazza di Spagna
and the Fontana della Barcaccia ('Fountain of the Ugly Boat') to
the Trinità dei Monti church at the top, they were designed,
following a competition, by Francesco de Sanctis (1679–1731) and
completed in 1725. The Spanish Steps became even more famous
after their appearance in the 1953 film, *Roman Holiday*, starring
Audrey Hepburn (1929–93) and Gregory Peck (1916–2003).

TEMPLE OF ESCULAPIO, VILLA BORGHESE

Rome, Italy

The Villa Borghese is a beautiful, large, landscaped park designed in the English manner. The garden contains a number of buildings, museums and other attractions, including the Temple of Esculapio, built purely as a landscape feature and influenced by the lake at the Stourhead estate in Wiltshire in England. The Piazza di Sienna, an amphitheatre used in May to host Rome's top equestrian event, can also be found there. Originally the seventeenth-century residence of Cardinal Scipione Borghese (1577–1633), the park and its spectacular gardens cover around 80 ha (198 ac).

COLOSSUS STATUE OF CONSTANTINE THE GREAT

Rome, Italy

Once to be found at the Basilica of Maxentius near the Forum Romanum, pieces of the Colossus are now located in the courtyard of the Palazzo dei Conservatori of the Musei Capitolini on the Capitoline Hill, above the Forum's west end. The Roman Forum, situated in the centre of the city, is one of the world's great tourist attractions. For centuries the epicentre of Roman life, the site of triumphal processions, elections, speeches, criminal trials, markets and gladiatorial combats, its sprawling ruins attract around 4.5 million visitors every year.

PYRAMID OF CESTIUS

Rome, Italy

The ancient Pyramid of Cestius stands close to the Porta San Paolo and Rome's Protestant cemetery. Built around 18–12 BC, as a tomb for the magistrate Gaius Cestius (d. AD 67), it is built of brick-faced concrete with slabs of white marble standing on foundations of Travertine limestone with an interior containing a burial chamber. Amongst the graves in the nearby Protestant cemetery are those of the Romantic poets John Keats (1795–1821), who died in Rome of tuberculosis aged 25, and Percy Bysshe Shelley (1792–1822), whose ashes were brought to Rome after his death by drowning.

PANORAMA OF THE VATICAN CITY

Rome, Italy

At just under half a kilometre square (0.3 sq m), the Vatican City is the world's smallest state but it is, nonetheless, packed with stunning treasures. The four Raphael Rooms offer the viewer a series of frescoes painted by the High Renaissance master for Pope Julius II (1443–1513), and there are art works from antiquity

to the Renaissance. The jewel in the crown, however, is the
extraordinary Sistine Chapel ceiling, with its magnificent frescoes
painted by Michelangelo (1475–1564), depicting Adam being
brought to life by just a touch of God's forefinger. Michelangelo
undertook his astonishing masterpiece between 1508 and 1512.

THE GREAT SYNAGOGUE

Florence, Italy

After centuries of persecution, Italian Jews finally gained emancipation in the second half of the nineteenth century, and the Great Synagogue (also known as the Tempio Maggiore) was a response to this new-found freedom. Built between 1874 and 1882, it was largely constructed using a donation by David Levi, a member of the Florentine Jewish community whose ambition was to build a synagogue that would match the beauty of other buildings in Florence. The result is a heady mix of Islamic, Jewish and Christian religious architecture, somewhat reminiscent of Hagia Sophia in Istanbul and no less stunning.

BARDINI GARDEN AND VIEW OF FLORENCE

Florence, Italy

The relatively unknown Bardini Garden offers one of the best views of the city of Florence. Situated in 4 ha (9.9 ac) of park between the left bank of the Arno River, the Montecuccoli Hill and the medieval walls, this Italian Renaissance garden was enlarged in 1700. In the nineteenth century, it was enhanced further with the addition of gardens in the Victorian style. Its rich array of flora and fauna, large baroque flight of steps and six fountains with mosaics and rose borders have all recently been restored to their original splendour.

SAN FREDIANO IN CESTELLO CHURCH

Florence, Italy

Like a number of other important churches in Florence, including the Duomo, the façade of San Frediano in Cestello was left unfinished. Nonetheless, this church provides one of the best examples of Florentine architecture of the late baroque period. Occupied in 1628 by the Cistercian monks from whom its name is derived, rebuilding began in 1680 and in 1689, its imposing cupola and bell tower were added. The interior of the church houses many works of art by some of the leading artists of the period, including Gabbiani (1652–1726), Dandini, Gherardini and Puglieschi (1660–1732).

BASILICA DI SANTA CROCE

Florence, Italy

Not for nothing is the Basilica di Santa Croce sometimes known as the Temple of Italian Glories, for it is the burial place of a number of notable Italians, including the artist Michelangelo, scientist and astronomer Galileo (1564–1642), politician and philosopher Niccolò Machiavelli (1469–1527), poet and revolutionary Ugo Foscolo (1778–1827) and composer Gioachino Rossini (1792–1868). The largest Franciscan church in the world, Santa Croce contains 16 chapels, many of which are decorated with frescoes by Giotto (1266/67–1337) and his pupils. Begun in 1294, the current church reflects the austere approach to life of the Franciscan order.

UFFIZI GALLERY

Florence, Italy

Designed by painter and architect Giorgio Vasari (1511–74) for Cosimo I de' Medici (1519–74), the Uffizi was originally built to accommodate the offices of Florentine magistrates, 'uffizi' translating as offices. After the fall of the House of Medici, the works of art collected by them remained there and in 1765, it was opened to the public as one of the first modern museums. Now one of the world's greatest, it houses a staggering collection of art including work by Duccio (d. 1319), Giotto, Ucello (1397–1475), Piero della Francesca (c. 1415–92), Botticelli (c. 1445–1510), Leonardo da Vinci (1452–1519), Dürer (1471–1528), Michelangelo and Rembrandt.

PALAZZO PITTI

Florence, Italy

The forbidding Renaissance Palazzo Pitti, situated on the south side of the River Arno, dates from 1458, when it was the residence of Florentine banker Luca Pitti (1398–1472). Purchased by the wealthy Medicis in 1549, it became the main residence of the ruling families of the Grand Duchy of Tuscany until 1860 and was later the principal royal palace of the united Italy. Donated to the Italian people by King Victor Emmanuel III (1869–1947) in 1919, the Pitti Palace is now the largest museum complex in Florence, with a collection of 250,000 works of art.

THE FOUNTAIN OF NEPTUNE

Florence, Italy

Often called 'Il Gigante' ('the giant') due to its great size, the Neptune Fountain was built 'to serve the people', as the inscription on its base states. Situated in front of the Palazzo Vecchio in the Piazza della Signore, the fountain was commissioned in 1565 for the wedding of Francesco I de' Medici (1541–87) and Johanna of Austria (1547–78), and built by Bartolomeo Ammannati. It was intended to allude to Florentine domination of the sea, but Florentines were unhappy with it, nicknaming it 'Il Biancone' ('the white giant').

THE BOBOLI GARDENS

Florence, Italy

Rising behind the Palazzo Pitti are the beautiful Boboli Gardens, one of the earliest examples of the sixteenth-century Italian Garden style that would influence the gardens of so many European courts, in particular Versailles. Originally designed for the wealthy and powerful Medici family, the park contains centuries-old oak trees and numerous sculptures and fountains. It is also home to a large amphitheatre on the hill behind the palace, the Viottolone sloping tree-lined avenue, the beautiful Giardino del Cavaliere and the splendid eighteenth-century Kaffeehaus.

SANTA MARIA DEL FIORE CATHEDRAL

Florence, Italy

The iconic Santa Maria del Fiore Catherdral, popularly known as Il Duomo di Firenze, was begun in 1296 and designed in the Gothic style by Italian architect and sculptor Arnolfo di Cambio (c. 1245–1301/10). With its breathtaking dome, a marvel of engineering designed by Filippo Brunelleschi (1377–1446), it was completed in 1436. The cathedral complex, situated in Piazza del Duomo, is also home to the Baptistery, constructed in the Romanesque style between 1059 and 1128 and the richly decorated 84.7 m (278 ft) high Campanile, designed by the great Italian medieval master, Giotto.

THE PONTE VECCHIO ON THE RIVER ARNO

Florence, Italy

The Ponte Vecchio, or 'Old Bridge', spanning the River Arno
at its lowest point, seems to belong to another age. Shops
stretch along its length, as was once common on bridges.
Initially these were butchers but they are now occupied by
jewellers, art dealers and sellers of gaudy souvenirs. Above the
main thoroughfare runs the Vasari Corridor, commissioned
by Cosimo I de' Medici to connect the Uffizi to the Pitti
Palace so that his family could make that journey without
having to mix with the ordinary people of Florence.

PIAZZA SAN MARCO

Venice, Italy

Overlooked by the ornate Italo-Byzantine Basilica San Marco and the Venetian Gothic Doge's Palace to which the basilica is connected, the great, wide square of San Marco is the main symbol of the city of Venice and its principal tourist attraction. The square's patterned floor is always thick with fluttering pigeons and expensive cafés line its edges under the balustrades. It is no wonder that Napoleon described Piazza San Marco as 'the finest drawing room in Europe', surely one of the best places on earth to sit and watch the world go by.

THE ART BLUE CAFÉ IN CAMPO SANTO STEFANO

Venice, Italy

Close to the Accademia Bridge lies the beautiful large square, Campo Santo Stefano, surrounded on all sides by lovely buildings, fascinating churches – including the fourteenth-century Chiesa di Santo Stefano – and tempting cafés and shops. Until the early nineteenth century, bullfights and bullbaiting were staged here, but nowadays it is the scene of outdoor fairs at Christmas and during Carnevale. Although not far from St Mark's Square, there is an entirely different atmosphere in Campo Santo Stefano and it is more likely to be frequented by strolling Venetians.

SCALA CONTARINI DEL BOVOLO

Venice, Italy

The Scala Contarini del Bovolo is a series of elegant arches lining an external spiral staircase in the small Palazzo Contarini del Bovolo that is situated in a quiet side street near the Campo Manin, close to the Rialto Bridge. At the top of the staircase is a splendid view out over the rooftops of Venice. The palace was built in the fifteenth century as one of the Venetian residences of the powerful Contarini family that provided no fewer than eight Doges to the Republic of Venice.

RIALTO BRIDGE

Venice, Italy

The Rialto Bridge is the most famous and the oldest of the four bridges that span the Grand Canal. Built by Antonio da Ponte (1512–95) between 1588 and 1591, it divides the districts of San Marco and San Polo, a spectacularly beautiful edifice that has become an architectural icon of the city. It is made up of two inclined ramps that lead to a central portico and on either side of the portico, the ramps are busy with shops and always teeming with tourists.

GRAND CANAL

Venice, Italy

Every day, the Grand Canal is thronged with water taxis, water buses, commercial vessels and, of course, gondolas bearing starry-eyed tourists. At one end, the canal feeds into the lagoon close to the city's railway station, Santa Lucia, while at the other, it flows into the San Marco Basin. Between these two points, it forms a large reverse S-shape through the centre of Venice. It is spanned by four bridges – the Rialto Bridge, the Ponte degli Scalzi, the Ponte dell'Accademia and the recently built and hugely controversial Ponte della Constituzione.

DORSODURO NEIGHBOURHOOD

Venice, Italy

The historic city of Venice is divided into six *sestieri,* or districts. These are Dorsoduro, Cannaregio, San Polo, Santa Croce, San Marco and Castello. Dorsoduro takes its name from the Italian for 'hard ridge' and, indeed, it is fortunate in this city of floods and sinking buildings to be built on comparatively high, stable land. In the nineteenth century, the Accademia di Belle Arti di Venezia – the academy of art – originally founded in 1750, was established in Dorsoduro and the Ponte dell'Accademia linked the area to San Marco.

CHURCH OF
PANAGHIA KAPNIKAREA

Athens, Greece

Probably built sometime in the eleventh century, the Greek
Orthodox Church of Panaghia Kapnikarea in the centre of
modern Athens is one of the oldest churches in the city and one
of its most important Byzantine monuments. As with other early
Christian churches, it was built on the site of an earlier Greek
pagan temple, in this case dedicated to the worship of a goddess
who is thought to have been either Athena or Demeter. Most
of the paintings inside the church are the work of the famous
modern Greek artist Photios Kontoglou (1895–1965).

THEATRE OF DIONYSUS

Athens, Greece

Often described as the birthplace of European drama, the open-
air Theatre of Dionysus lies in a natural setting on the southern
slopes of the Acropolis at Athens. The world's first theatre built
of stone, it was the stage for the dramatic contests of the festivals
held in honour of the god Dionysus, and in the fifth century
BC, the plays of the great Greek dramatists Aeschylus (*c.* 525
–456 BC), Sophocles (*c.* 496–406 BC), Euripides (*c.* 480–406
BC) and Aristophanes (*c.* 446–c. 386 BC) received their first
performances here. Today's remains date to Roman times, when
the theatre could seat an audience of around 17,000.

ACROPOLIS OF ATHENS

Athens, Greece

Appropriately, Acropolis means 'topmost part of the city', as it rises to 156 m (512 ft) above the city of Athens. It is naturally fortified with sheer drops on three of its sides, meaning that it can only be accessed from the west. Settled as early as 3000 BC, the Acropolis gradually became a place of worship, and during the Archaic Period, between 800 and 480 BC, became the sanctuary of the goddess Athena. It is now a monument to the achievements of the Ancient Greeks and one of the world's most visited tourist destinations.

PITTAKI STREET

Athens, Greece

Despite Greece's recent financial problems, Athens remains a vibrant, exciting city. One example of this can be found in Pittaki Street, a dimly lit, neglected alley until the urban lightscape design group Before Light decided to do something about it. They searched out all the old lampshades they could find – from chandeliers to shantung-covered shades, bell shades to Chinese paper lanterns – rewired and weatherproofed them and hung them in glowing lines along the length of the street. Tourists now flock to this once-neglected thoroughfare and smile.

MIKROLIMANO MARINA IN PIRAEUS

Athens, Greece

Piraeus was largely developed in the fifth century BC, when it became the seaport serving Athens, developing into the principal port for Ancient Greece. Having declined from the fourth century AD, it rose to prominence once more in 1834 when Athens again became the capital of the Kingdom of Greece following independence from the Ottoman Empire. Mikrolimano is the second largest marina of modern Piraeus, attracting tourists and Athenians alike to dine at its fabulous restaurants and taverns while watching fishing boats and luxury yachts bob on the waves in its beautiful harbour.

PARTHENON

Athens, Greece

The nineteenth-century French engineer Auguste Choisy (1841–1909), described the Parthenon as 'the supreme effort of genius in pursuit of beauty'. But we can only imagine how this amazing building must have looked in the middle of the fifth century BC, where worshippers gathered in its towering central sanctuary, adoring a 12.2 m (40 ft) statue of the goddess Athena. The Parthenon represents the zenith of Classical Greek achievement, an enduring symbol of not just that period but also of Athenian democracy and Western civilization. Begun in 447 BC, it was completed nine years later.

ATHENS NATIONAL GARDEN

Athens, Greece

This oasis in the middle of Athens provides respite from the heat, noise and bustle of the busy city. Located directly behind the Greek Parliament building, the Athens National Garden – formerly the Royal Garden – extends to the south, where the Zappeion building sits across from the Panathenaiko Olympic stadium, site of the 1896 Olympic Games. The garden contains ancient ruins, Corinthian capitals, mosaics and many other features, including busts of famous Greeks. In the 1920s, the park was opened to the public and renamed the National Garden.

ACROPOLIS

ANAFIOTIKA, PLAKA

Athens, Greece

Plaka is an old Athenian neighbourhood, known as the 'Neighbourhood of the Gods' due to its proximity to the Acropolis. Built on top of the residential areas of the ancient town of Athens, its labyrinthine streets – many closed to vehicles – cluster around the northern and eastern slopes of the Acropolis complex. Every year it is visited by hundreds of thousands of tourists, who have a wide range of attractions to entice them, including museums, souvenir shops, restaurants and cafés.

MOUNT LYCABETTUS

Athens, Greece

In Greek mythology, Lycabettus was created by the goddess Athena when she dropped a mountain she was carrying for the building of the Acropolis. In reality, it is a 300 m (984 ft) high Cretaceous limestone hill in the middle of Athens whose name translates as 'the one [hill] that is walked by wolves'. At the top of the hill – accessed by a funicular railway – stands the nineteenth-century Chapel of St George, a restaurant and a large open-air theatre that has hosted concerts for everyone from Bob Dylan to Black Sabbath.

MONASTERY IN MESSARA VALLEY

Crete, Greece

The stunning beauty of the island of Crete is matched by the wealth of its history. It was once the centre of the Minoan civilization, Europe's earliest recorded advanced civilization, that survived from *c.* 2700–1420 BC. It was a time rich in myth and legend, when Theseus stalked the Minotaur and the Minoans ruled most of the Aegean. Ancient treasures and vestiges of the island's past are everywhere, including the ancient settlement of Knossos, regarded as Europe's oldest city, but there are also sun-drenched beaches, dreamy villages and breathtaking landscapes to be enjoyed.

LEFKA ORI MOUNTAINS

Crete, Greece

The western province of Sfakia stretches from the Omalos Plateau down to the southern coast of the island. In this area can be found some of Crete's most spectacular sights, including the Lefka Ori Mountains – or White Mountains – whose highest peak rises to 2,453 m (8,048 ft), and which include the stunning Samaria Gorge and the rugged Mount Gingilos, with its impressive vertical north face and stunning views of the Aegean Sea, the north coast of the island, and the Libyan Sea stretching to the North African coast to the south.

KNOSSOS PALACE

Crete, Greece

The Bronze Age ruins of the palace at Knossos were uncovered in 1900 by the British archaeologist, Sir Arthur Evans (1851–1941). His first discoveries, such as the Throne Room and a fresco of a Minoan man, stunned an archaeological world surprised by the fact that a civilization of such maturity could have existed at the time when the pharaohs ruled Egypt. Some even speculated that it might be the lost city of Atlantis. The splendour of Knossos and the Minoan Civilization is evident in the palace's elegant frescoes and decorations.

SAMARIA GORGE

Crete, Greece

The Samaria Gorge is a hugely popular tourist destination situated in the National Park of Samaria in the Lefka Ori Mountains in the west of Crete. This majestic 16 km (10 m) long gorge starts at an altitude of 1,250 metres at its northern entrance before descending to the shores of the Libyan Sea at the village of Agia Roumeli. At the gorge's most famous section, the Gates, its sides close in to a width of just 4 m (13 ft) and soar up to almost 300 m (984 ft).

AGIOS NIKOLAOS

Crete, Greece

East of Heraklion, capital of Crete, on the shores of the gorgeous Mirabello Bay, lies the modern coastal resort of Agios Nikolaos. From the town's harbour, a narrow channel dug in 1870 leads into the beautiful lagoon of Voulismeni Lake in which, according to legend, the

goddess Athena bathed, but which is now lined with cafés
and restaurants. By night, the harbour side comes alive as stylish
young Greeks stroll in the evening sun and holidaymakers
come into town from the surrounding villages to eat, drink
and watch the sun go down.

MONASTERY OF ARKADI GARDEN

Crete, Greece

With its unique natural beauty, rich history and wealth of legend, the Orthodox Arkadi Monastery is one of the most important destinations on Crete, the current church dating back to the sixteenth century and showing the influence of the Renaissance in its architectural style which mixes both Roman and baroque elements. The monastery became a symbol of Greek national resistance when, during the Cretan revolt of 1866–69, many Greeks, mostly women and children, sought refuge there. After battling for three days, they chose to blow themselves up rather than surrender.

MATALA BEACH AND CAVES, NEAR HERAKLION

Crete, Greece

According to legend, Matala is the place where the god Zeus swam ashore in the shape of a bull with Europa on his back. Things were different in the 1960s, however, when Matala was home to a colony of hippies who were attracted by the free accommodation provided by the caves that had been hewn out of the cliffs by Neolithic peoples. The period is remembered by one of them, Canadian singer Joni Mitchell (b. 1943) who, in her song *Carey* (1971), sings '… they're playin' that scratchy rock and roll/Beneath the Matala Moon'.

MEDUSA COLUMN IN THE BASILICA CISTERN

Istanbul, Turkey

Beneath the streets of Istanbul lie several hundred ancient cisterns of which the Basilica Cistern is the largest. Located 150 m (492 ft) south-west of Hagia Sophia, and built in the sixth century, the cistern provided a water filtration system for the Great Palace of Constantinople and other buildings and continued to provide water for the Topkapi Palace into modern times. The bases of two columns located in the north-west corner of the cistern reuse blocks carved with the face of Medusa, thought to have been borrowed from a building of the late Roman period.

SÜLEYMANIYE MOSQUE

Istanbul, Turkey

One of the best-known sights of the city of Istanbul is the magnificent Süleymaniye Mosque. The city's largest mosque, it was built by the architectural genius Mimar Sinan (*c.* 1490–1588) on the orders of Sultan Süleyman 'the Magnificent' (1495–1566). Work commenced in 1550 and it was finished in 1558. The interior of the mosque, a near-square measuring 58 x 59 m (190 x 194 ft), is simply breathtaking in size and in atmosphere. The mosque complex includes a Turkish bath, a restaurant serving fine Ottoman cuisine, theological colleges, a hospital, schools and a hostel for travellers.

THE BOSPHORUS BRIDGE

Istanbul, Turkey

Completed in 1973, the Bosphorus Bridge is one of two
bridges that span the Bosphorus, connecting Europe with
Asia, the other being the Fatih Sultan Mehmed Bridge,
opened in 1988. The notion of such a bridge dates back to
antiquity but it took until 1957 for the project to be given
the go-ahead. It was designed by the renowned British civil
engineers, Sir Gilbert Roberts (1899–1978) and William
Brown (1928–2005), designers of the Forth Road Bridge
and many others, and opened to mark the 50th anniversary
of the Republic of Turkey.

SULTAN AHMED MOSQUE

Istanbul, Turkey

Originally known as the Blue Mosque because of the 20,000 shimmering blue tiles that adorn the walls of its interior, the Sultan Ahmed Mosque was built by Sedefkâr Mehmed Ağa (1540–1617) during the sultanate of Ahmed I (1590–1617). Completed in 1616 on the site of the Great Palace of Constantinople, this most photogenic of buildings is one of two mosques in Turkey that has six minarets and its courtyard is the largest of the Ottoman mosques. The interior is vast with 260 windows spraying light down on to the carpeted floor below.

THE GRAND BAZAAR

Istanbul, Turkey

Chaos reigns in the colourful, bustling Grand Bazaar in the heart of Istanbul's Old City. One of the largest and oldest covered markets in the world, it was opened on the orders of Sultan Mehmed II (1432–81) in 1461 as a small warehouse for trading textiles. Its 61 labyrinthine, covered streets and over 3,000 shops now place it amongst the world's most visited tourist attractions, with more than 91 million visitors a year, who can try out the art of haggling, drink tea and watch artisans ply their crafts.

HAGIA SOPHIA

Istanbul, Turkey

Of all the superb and important monuments that Istanbul offers the visitor, it is unlikely that any surpasses Hagia Sophia. Commissioned in 532 by the Byzantine emperor Justinian (482–565), consecrated as a church in 537 and converted to a mosque by Sultan Mehmed II in 1453, its religious significance, rich history, architectural qualities and, above all, its extraordinary beauty make it very special. In the interior light famously reflects everywhere, making it appear as if its massive dome, a miracle of engineering when it was built, is floating above the nave.

DOLMABAHÇE CLOCK TOWER

Istanbul, Turkey

Dolmabahçe Palace is the largest of the imperial palaces on the Bosphorus. Constructed by Abdülmecid I (1823–61) between 1843 and 1856, the palace is built in a European baroque, rococo and imperial style on three storeys and has 285 rooms, 46 halls, 6 Turkish baths and 68 toilets. It is said that 40 tons of silver and 14 tons of gold were used in decorating it. The four-sided, four-storey, 27 m (89 ft) high clock tower was designed between 1890 and 1895 in Ottoman neo-baroque style by court architect Sarkis Balyan (1835–99).

RUMELI FORTRESS

Istanbul, Turkey

Built by Sultan Mehmed II in a remarkable four months in
1451 and 1452, on the European side of the Bosphorus in
preparation for his siege and capture of Constantinople, the
imposing Rumeli Hisari is situated at the narrowest point on
the Bosphorus. It stands opposite Anadolu Hisari on the
Anatolian side, built in 1394 by Sultan Beyazit I (1360–1403),
and allowed Mehmed to control all the traffic on the strait,
preventing Constantinople from being resupplied from the
Black Sea during the 1453 siege of the city.

CHORA CHURCH

Istanbul, Turkey

The fresco-laden Church of the Holy Saviour in Chora is
considered by many to be one of the most beautiful surviving
examples of a Byzantine church and second only to Hagia
Sophia. Originally built in the fifth century as part of a
monastery complex south of the Golden Horn, its name
referred to its location outside the walls of Constantinople
('chora' literally means 'country'). Rebuilt at least five times,
most of the interior decoration, including the famous mosaics
and the frescoes, date to 1312 and were funded by poet and
government official, Theodore Metochites (c. 1270–1332).

CENTRAL AND EASTERN EUROPE

Central and Eastern Europe were of course for decades very much off the tourist trail, as some of the nations struggled under the yoke of communism. Since the fall of the Berlin Wall in 1989, however, the region's treasures have once again become available to all – magnificent castle fortresses, medieval town quarters, Gothic and baroque churches, sights and sounds from other ages, all accessible with a quick and often relatively inexpensive flight.

Indeed, many of the towns and cities of Central and Eastern Europe have been spared the blight of modernization and urban development, with Budapest, for example, used as a stand-in for many other cities in films. So far, it has masqueraded as London (*Being Julia*, 2004), Buenos Aires (*Evita*, 1996), Moscow (*A Good Day to Die Hard*, 2013) and Berlin (*The Boy in the Striped Pyjamas*, 2008), amongst others. Less familiar to the visitor than, say, the attractions of Rome or Paris, there is still much to impress in the sights of Prague and Budapest, such as the striking Charles Bridge in Prague or the faintly bizarre Memento Park in Budapest. Vienna, of course, is a magnificent city we associate with the waltz and fabulous history. Its palaces and museums are second to none.

VRTBOVSKÁ GARDEN

Prague, Czech Republic

The Czech baroque style of architecture was unique to the regions of Bohemia, Moravia and Czech Silesia in the seventeenth and eighteenth centuries and can be seen not just in the towns and cities but also in the Czech countryside, where churches and chapels are mostly built in this style. In Prague, there are several high baroque terraced gardens, one of which is the Vrtbovská Garden, in the Lesser Town. Built for Jan Josef, Count of Vrtba, this spectacular masterpiece of garden design provides a feast for the eyes.

CHARLES BRIDGE

Prague, Czech Republic

Prague's most stunning bridge spans 16 arches and is lined with 30 baroque statues of religious figures erected between 1683 and 1714. Originally known as the 'Stone Bridge', it was commissioned in 1357 by Charles IV, King of Bohemia and Holy Roman Emperor, and until 1841 was the only means of crossing the River Vltava. It stretches for 520 m (1,706 ft) across the Vltava, is 10 m (33 ft) wide and is protected by three towers, the one on the Old Town side recognized as one of the most accomplished civil Gothic style buildings in the world.

PRAGUE CASTLE

Prague, Czech Republic

Prague Castle, with its spires, towers and palaces, looks like a page torn out of a book of fairy tales, looming above the left bank of the Vltava and dominating the city's skyline. The largest ancient castle in the world, at 570 m (1,870 ft) long and 128 m (420 ft) wide, it covers the equivalent of seven football pitches. The first fortified settlement on the site was created in the ninth century and since then, it has been added to by the rulers who lived there, leading to an eclectic variety of architectural styles.

FRANZ KAFKA STATUE IN THE JEWISH QUARTER

Prague, Czech Republic

Jaroslav Rona's (b. 1957) bronze statue of the novelist and short-story writer, Franz Kafka (1883–1924), stands in a little square in the middle of Dusni Street in Prague's Jewish Quarter. Kafka lived in the Jewish Quarter all his life and the square is what he would have seen every time he looked out the window of his room. The sculpture of a headless male figure in a suit with a smaller figure of Kafka sitting on his shoulders is inspired by one of the writer's short stories, *Description of a Struggle* (published posthumously in 1936).

JUBILEE SYNAGOGUE

Prague, Czech Republic

Prague's Jubilee Synagogue, with its exuberantly colourful façade, was built in 1906, the youngest synagogue in the city but also the largest. Designed by renowned Viennese architect, Wilhelm Stiassny (1842–1910), in the Art Nouveau style of the time, with pseudo-Moorish elements, the synagogue took its name from the 50th anniversary of the ascension to the Austro-Hungarian throne of Emperor Franz Josef I (1830–1916). The synagogue houses an exhibition of artefacts, photographs and films that chart the history of Prague's Jewish community following the horrors of the Second World War.

HAVEL'S MARKET

Prague, Czech Republic

A stroll through Prague's beautiful Old Town uncovers many of the city's treasures – the Art Nouveau decor of the Municipal House, the Gothic Powder Gate and the rococo splendour of the Kinsky Palace, home to part of the National Museum's modern art collection. You might also stumble upon Havel's Market, which dates back to 1232 and is one of the oldest of the city's markets. A number of the stalls sell souvenirs but others offer inexpensive handmade Czech crystal and glass jewellery, tasty traditional spa wafers, local honey and delightful wooden toys.

CHAPEL OF THE HOLY SEPULCHRE ON PETŘÍN HILL

Prague, Czech Republic

Petřín Park, situated close to Prague Castle, is an ideal place to relax or spend a quiet afternoon. There are several holy monuments there, one of which is the charming baroque Chapel of the Holy Sepulchre, built in 1737 in imitation of a small chapel in Jerusalem. Standing close to the Cathedral of St Lawrence, the chapel contains a window positioned in such a way that a beam of sunlight will fall on the sacrificial stone in the centre of the chapel.

ASTRONOMICAL CLOCK IN THE OLD TOWN SQUARE

Prague, Czech Republic

Situated in Prague's Old Town Quarter, the wonderful Old Town Square has remained almost unchanged since the tenth century. At the centre is the Jan Hus (*c.* 1369–1415) statue, erected in 1915 to mark the 500th anniversary of the death of the great Czech Church reformer. The Astronomical Clock is a medieval clock, first installed on the southern wall of the Old Town Hall in the square in 1410. It is the third oldest such clock in the world and the oldest one still in working order.

CHURCH OF OUR LADY BEFORE TÝN

Prague, Czech Republic

The fifteenth-century Church of Our Lady Before Týn, with its distinctive, Disney-like Gothic twin spires, rises dramatically behind the four-storey Týn School, looking down on Prague's delightful and historic Old Town Square. The church is undeniably Gothic on the outside but its interior is decidedly baroque. It contains the tomb of the Danish astronomer Tycho Brahe (1546–1601) and on the inside of the southern wall are two blocked off windows that once opened into the church from rooms where the teenage Franz Kafka lived from 1896 to 1907.

VIEW OF BUDA SIDE OF BUDAPEST WITH BUDA CASTLE, MATTHIAS CHURCH AND FISHERMAN'S BASTION

Budapest, Hungary

Budapest's Castle Hill, with its numerous attractions, is one of the jewels in the crown of this wonderful city, undeniably one of the most beautiful places in Europe. The castle is built on the southern tip of Castle Hill next to the Castle Quarter with its medieval, baroque and nineteenth-century churches, houses and public buildings replete with history and charm. Castle Hill offers much to see apart from the magnificent castle, such as the 700-year-old Matthias Church, and the neogothic Fisherman's Bastion, providing panoramic views of the splendours of Budapest.

VAJDAHUNYAD CASTLE

Budapest, Hungary

Situated in Budapest's City Park, Vajdahunyad Castle was built between 1896 and 1908 as part of the city's millennial exhibition celebrating the 1000th anniversary of the settlement of the Hungarian people in Central Europe. Hungarian architect Ignác Alpár (1855–1928) designed this extraordinary edifice with copies of elements from important Hungarian buildings, giving it a variety of architectural styles – Romanesque, Gothic, Renaissance and baroque. It was originally constructed in cardboard and wood for the exhibition but proved so popular that it was rebuilt in stone and brick.

HEROES' SQUARE

Budapest, Hungary

The imposing statue complex featuring the Seven Chieftains of the Magyars, important national leaders and the Tomb of the Unknown Soldier, dominates Heroes Square, one of the major squares in the city of Budapest. Lying at the end of the grand boulevard of Andrássy Avenue next to City Park, the square is home to the eclectic neoclassical-styled Museum of Fine Arts and Hall of Art. It has been the scene of many important political events, such as the re-internment in 1989 of the executed hero of the 1956 Hungarian Revolution, Imre Nagy (1896–1958).

SZÉCHENYI SPA BATHS

Budapest, Hungary

Hungary is the country of baths, the Romans having built the first spas there, followed in the sixteenth century by the country's Turkish occupiers who built Turkish baths in Budapest. But, with its neo-baroque palace, there is no spa in the world as grand as the Széchenyi Spa Baths in Budapest's City Park. Planned since the 1880s but finally opened in 1913, it now boasts three outdoor and 15 indoor pools. In its first year, it was used by more than 200,000 health-seekers, but by 1919 almost 900,000 people were bathing there every year.

PARLIAMENT BUILDING

Budapest, Hungary

The beautiful Gothic Revival Hungarian Parliament is the most outstanding landmark on the Pest side of the Danube. Built to celebrate the nation's 1000th anniversary in 1896, it was finally completed in 1904, architect Imre Steindl (1839–1902) partly inspired by the Palace of Westminster which had only recently been completed. Ornamented with graceful neogothic turrets and arches, the building stretches for 268 m (880 ft) along the Danube and incorporates 20 k (12.5 m) of corridors, 691 rooms and a 96 m (315 ft) high central dome. Statues of Hungarian monarchs and soldiers decorate the outer walls.

FISHERMAN'S BASTION

Budapest, Hungary

The terrace of Fisherman's Bastion in Budapest rises in neogothic and neo-Romanesque splendour above the Buda bank of the Danube on Castle Hill. Designed and built between 1895 and 1902, its towers and terrace provide breathtaking panoramic views of the Danube, Margaret Island, Pest to the east and Gellért Hill. The Bastion's name is derived from the guild of fishermen whose responsibility it was in the Middle Ages to defend this stretch of the city walls against invasion and its seven towers represent the seven Magyar tribes that conquered Hungary in 896.

STATUES IN MEMENTO PARK

Budapest, Hungary

Memento Park, 10 km (6.2 m) south–west of Budapest city centre, is a unique outdoor museum that remembers Hungary's communist past (1949–89). It contains around 40 statues, busts and plaques of the former heroes of communism – Marx, Engels, Lenin, the Hungarian revolutionary Béla Kun, and others. In other countries such artefacts were destroyed but in Budapest they are exhibited to serve as a reminder of troubled times. An exhibition centre presents displays explaining the failed 1956 Hungarian Revolution and there is rare footage of secret agents collecting information on 'subversives'.

ST STEPHEN'S BASILICA

Budapest, Hungary

Budapest's neoclassical Roman Catholic cathedral, St Stephen's Basilica, is named for Stephen, first King of Hungary (975–1038), who ruled from *c.* 1000–38. His mummified right hand that is housed in the church's reliquary was discovered in a monastery in Bosnia, and returned to Hungary by Habsburg empress, Maria Theresa (1717–80) in 1771. Completed in 1905, the basilica took 50 years to build, mainly because the dome collapsed in a storm in 1868, after which the structure had to be demolished and entirely rebuilt.

SZÉCHENYI CHAIN BRIDGE

Budapest, Hungary

The twin-towered span of the Széchenyi Chain Bridge in the centre of Budapest is one of the most beautiful bridges across the River Danube. Designed by the English civil engineer, William Tierney Clark (1783–1852), who also designed London's Hammersmith Bridge in 1827, it was regarded at the time as one of the engineering world's modern wonders and with a central span of 202 m (663 ft), was one of the largest on earth. When it opened in 1849, the Chain Bridge was the first permanent dry link between the two halves of the city, Buda and Pest.

ST CHARLES'S CHURCH

Vienna, Austria

The finest and most dramatic of Vienna's baroque churches,
St Charles's Church – or Karlskirche – was built between
1716 and 1739. It was the product of a vow by Holy Roman
Emperor Charles VI (1685–1740) after the great plague
epidemic of 1712 to build a church dedicated to the Italian
St Charles Borromeo, who was revered as a healer for those
suffering from plague. Designed and begun by Austrian
architect, Johann Bernhard Fischer von Erlach (1656–1723),
it was completed by his son Joseph Emanuel (1693–1742).
The church's impressive oval dome is 72 m (236 ft) high.

JOHANN STRAUSS IN STADTPARK

Vienna, Austria

Vienna's Stadtpark provides a peaceful escape from the noise of
the city with its quiet, winding paths and duck ponds lined with
beautiful willow trees. Through its 11.3 ha (28 ac) flows the
Wienfluss (River Wien) and scattered throughout the park are a
number of statues of famous Viennese artists, writers and musicians
including the painters Hans Canon (1829–85) and Emil Jakob
Schindler (1842–92), and musicians Franz Schubert (1797–1828),
Anton Bruckner (1824–96) and Josef Strauss II (1825–99).
Occasionally, the music of the waltz drifts across the park from
the opulent Kursalon building, where concerts are staged.

SCHÖNBRUNN PALACE

Vienna, Austria

With origins in a mansion called Katterburg, erected in 1548, this former Habsburg imperial summer residence gives a fascinating insight into the grandeur and opulence of the baroque period. The property was remodelled and rebuilt in the 1740s and 1750s during the reign of Empress Maria Theresa (1717–80), and Franz I (1830–1916) commissioned the neoclassical exterior that survives to this day. With the downfall of the Habsburgs in November 1918 after the First World War, the palace was turned into a museum and 40 of its 1,441 rooms are now open to visitors.

BELVEDERE PARK

Vienna, Austria

Belvedere Park, with its exquisite gardens, created in the Formal French style with gravelled walks and water features, is the location of one of the world's finest baroque palaces, Belvedere. Built for Prince Eugene of Savoy (1663–1736), it was designed by Austrian baroque architect, Johann Lukas von Hildebrandt (1668–1745), and completed in 1723. The Unteres (Lower) Belvedere has an orangery attached and was used as a summer residence by the prince, while in the Oberes (Upper) Belvedere, connected by a long, beautifully landscaped garden, the prince hosted banquets and parties.

WIENER STAATSOPER

Vienna, Austria

Designed in the neo-Renaissance style by the famous Czech architect, Josef Hlavka (1831–1908), the Staatsoper opera house was completed in 1869, although it was reportedly viewed as insufficiently grand by the people of Vienna. In fact, at the time it was dubbed '"the Königgrätz" of architecture', Königgrätz being a disastrous battle fought by the Austrians. After the auditorium and stage were destroyed by bombs in the Second World War, the opera house was rebuilt and it opened in 1955. Now it is one of the busiest and most famous opera houses in the world, staging 50 to 60 operas a year.

ST STEPHEN'S CATHEDRAL

Vienna, Austria

Stephansdom, or 'Steffi' as it is known to the Viennese, is a
Gothic masterpiece begun in 1359. It has a spectacularly tiled
roof, the tiles above the choir forming a mosaic of a double-
headed eagle, the Imperial symbol. Inside, the magnificent
1515 Gothic stone pulpit dominates the main nave while the
baroque high altar depicts the stoning of St Stephen, the
chancel on its left featuring the 1447 winged Wiener Neustadt
altarpiece, composed of two extraordinary triptychs. The funeral
of Venetian composer Antonio Vivaldi (1678–1741) was held in
the cathedral in 1741.

HUNDERTWASSER HOUSE

Vienna, Austria

The Viennese apartment block, Hundertwasser House, was conceived
by Austrian artist and architect, Friedensreich Hundertwasser
(1928–2000) who championed the idea of an architecture in
harmony with nature and man. He was invited in 1977 to create an
apartment building and, working with another architect Josef
Krawina (b. 1928), devised this extraordinary building with its
undulating floors, trees growing inside rooms, a forested roof terrace,
primary colours and sensuously curved lines. This iconic, much-loved
building houses 52 apartments, four offices, 16 private terraces and
three communal terraces, and a total of 250 trees and bushes.

MUSEUM OF NATURAL HISTORY

Vienna, Austria

Home to some 30 million objects and artefacts, the elaborate palace of the NHMW, as it is known, opened to the public in 1889. Amongst its collections are many rare and famous exhibits such as the Venus of Willendorf, a small statuette of a woman made between 28,000 and 25,000 BC, and her sister exhibit, the Venus of Galgenberg, at 34,000 years old the oldest figurative sculpture in existence. There are minerals and meteorites, and zoology and anthropology are well represented in the museum's extensive collections.

INDEX

Acropolis of Athens, Athens, Greece 132
Aeschylus 130
Agios Nikolaos, Crete, Greece 7, 144–145
Alfama house, Lisbon, Portugal 88–89
Alpár, Ignác 171
Ammannati, Bartolomeo 117
Amsterdam, The Netherlands 60–65
Anafiotika, Plaka, Athens, Greece 138–139
Anne Frank Statue, near the Anne
    Frank Museum, Amsterdam,
    The Netherlands 62
Arc de Triomf, Barcelona, Spain 76–77
Arnolfo di Cambio 118
Art Blue Café in Campo Santo Stefano,
    Venice, Italy 122–123
Arthur's Seat and Edinburgh cityscape,
    Edinburgh, Scotland 38–39
Astronomical Clock in the Old Town
    Square, Prague, Czech Republic 168–169
Athens, Greece 130–139
    Athens National Garden 136–137

Baldwin, James 9
Balyan, Sarkis 155
Barcelona, Spain 67, 68–81
    Barcelona Beach 70–71
Bardini Garden and view of Florence,
    Florence, Italy 110–111
Barrie, J.M. Peter Pan 25
Barry, Sir Charles 34
Basilica di Santa Croce, Florence, Italy 114
Baudelaire, Charles 18
Beckett, Samuel 48
Beethoven, Ludvig von 55
Being Julia 159
Belvedere Park, Vienna, Austria 184
Berlin, Germany 11, 52–59
    Berlin Cathedral 52–53
    Berlin Wall 57
Bernini, Gian Lorenzo 100
Bica Funicular, near Bairro Alto, Lisbon,
    Portugal 90
Big Ben and the Houses of Parliament,
    London, England 34–35
Boboli Garden, Florence, Italy 118
Book of Kells 47
Bosphorus Bridge, Istanbul, Turkey
    7, 150–151

Botticelli, Alessandro 114
Boy in the Striped Pyjamas, The 159
Brahe, Tycho 169
Brown, Dan The Da Vinci Code 18
Brown, William 151
Bruckner, Anton 181
Brunelleschi, Filippo 118
Budapest, Hungary 159
    Buda side of Budapest with Buda Castle,
        Matthias Church and Fisherman's
        Bastion 170–171

Café at Rue Mouffetard, Paris,
    France 14–15
Calatrava, Santiago 48
Campo Santo Stefano, Venice, Italy
    7, 122–123
Canon, Hans 181
Caravaggio, Michelangelo 86, 97
Carrer del Bisbe, Gothic Quarter,
    Barcelona, Spain 76
Cathedral Santa Maria del Fiore,
    Florence, Italy 118–119
Centre of Barcelona, Barcelona,
    Spain 78–79
Cervantes, Miguel Don Quixote 71, 90
Cézanne, Paul 17
Chapel of the Holy Sepulchre on Pet
    Ín Hill, Prague, Czech Republic
    166–167
Charles Bridge, Prague, Czech
    Republic 160–161
Charlottenburg Palace, Berlin, Germany
    7, 56–57
Château de Vincennes, Paris, France
    6–7, 14
Choisy, Auguste 136
Chora Church, Istanbul, Turkey 157
Christ Church Cathedral, Dublin,
    Ireland 50–51
Church of Our Lady Before Týn, Prague,
    Czech Republic 169
Church of Panaghia Kapnikarea,
    Athens, Greece 130
Cibeles Fountain, Madrid, Spain 82–83
Clark, William Tierney 178
Clusius, Carolus 61
Colosseum, Rome, Italy 96–97

Colossus Statue of Constantine the
    Great, Rome, Italy 106
Conran, Sir Terence 43
Crete, Greece 6, 95, 140–147
Crystal Palace in Retiro Park,
    Madrid, Spain 84–85

Dalí, Salvador 23, 84
Dandini, Pier 113
Dean Gallery, Edinburgh, Scotland 41
Delacroix, Eugène 18
Diageo Claive Vidiz Whisky Collection 39
Dolce Vita, La 103
Dolmabahçe Clock Tower, Istanbul,
    Turkey 155
Dorsoduro Neighbourhood, Venice,
    Italy 128–129
Doyle, Sir Arthur Conan 30
Dublin, Ireland 6, 11, 44–51
Duccio 114
Dürer, Albrecht 114

Edinburgh, Scotland 36–43
    Edinburgh Castle 6, 39, 40–41
Eiffel Tower, Paris, France 20–21, 28
Estonia 8
Euripides 130
Europe 6–9, 11, 67, 95, 159
Evans, Sir Arthur 143
Evita 159

Fischer von Erlach, Johann Bernard 181
Fischer von Erlach, Joseph Emmanuel 181
Fisherman's Bastion, Budapest, Hungary
    170–171, 176–177
Florence, Italy 95, 110–121
Foscolo, Ugo 114
Foster, Sir Norman 53
Fountain of Neptune, Florence, Italy 117
Frampton, Sir George 25
Frank, Anne 62
Franz Kafka Statue in the Jewish Quarter,
    Prague, Czech Republic 164

Gabbiani, Antonio 113
Galileo Galilei 114
Gama, Vasco da 67, 93
Gaudí, Antoni 67, 73, 74, 78

Gaudí Chimney at Casa Milà,
    Barcelona, Spain 81
Gaudí's Casa Batlló, Barcelona, Spain 68
Gehry, Frank 71
Gherardini, Alessandro 113
Giotto 114, 118
Good Day to Die Hard, A 159
Goya, Francisco 82, 86
Grand Bazaar, Istanbul, Turkey 153
Grand Canal, Venice, Italy 126–127
Great Synagogue, Florence, Italy 110
Güell, Eusebi 74

Hadrian's Villa, Rome, Italy 98–99
Hagia Sophia, Istanbul, Turkey 154–155
Hals, Frans 61
Hamilton, Thomas 41
Harry Potter and the Philosopher's Stone 30
Haus der Kulturen der Welt, Berlin,
    Germany 54–55
Havel's Market, Prague, Czech
    Republic 166
Haydn, Franz Joseph 55
Hemingway, Ernest The Sun Also Rises 82
Heroes' Square, Budapest, Hungary
    172–173
Hildebrandt, Johann Lukas von 184
Hlavka, Josef 184
Horn, Rebecca 71
Hugo, Victor 18
Hundertwasser House, Vienna, Austria 187
Hundertwasser, Friedensreich 187
Hus, Jan 169

Istanbul, Turkey 6, 148–157
Italian Gardens, Kensington Gardens,
    London, England 32–33

Jerónimos Monastery, Lisbon,
    Portugal 92–93
Johann Strauss in Stadtpark, Vienna,
    Austria 181
Jones, Inigo 33
Jones, Sir Horace 30
Jubilee Synagogue, Prague, Czech
    Republic 164–165
Juvara, Filippo 86

Kafka, Franz 164, 169
Keats, John 106
Kemp, George Meikle 36
Kew Gardens, London, England 28
Knossos Palace, Crete, Greece 142–143
Kontoglou, Photios 130
Krawina, Josef 187
Kun, Béla 177

La Boqueria Market, Barcelona,
    Spain 72–73
Lake at Farmleigh, Dublin, Ireland 44–45
Leadenhall Market, London, England 30
Lefka Ori Mountains, Crete, Greece
    140–141
Leith Harbour, Edinburgh, Scotland 42–43
Leonardo da Vinci 11, 17, 114
Lisbon, Portugal 67, 88–93
London, England 11, 24–35
Louvre, Paris, France 11, 16–17

Macchiavelli, Niccolò 114
Madrid, Spain 6, 67, 82–87
Matala Beach and Caves, near Heraklion,
    Crete, Greece 147
Matisse, Henri 17
Medici family 95, 114, 117, 118, 120
Medusa Column in the Basilica Cistern,
    Istanbul, Turkey 148–149
Mesnier de Ponsard, Raoul 90
Metochites, Theodore 157
Michelangelo 109, 114
Mikrolimano Marina in Piraeus,
    Athens, Greece 7, 134–135
Modern EYE Film Institute by the IJ
    Harbour, Amsterdam, The Netherlands
    62–63
Monastery in Messara Valley, Crete,
    Greece 140
Monastery of Arkadi Garden, Crete,
    Greece 146–147
Monet, Claude 17, 23
Montmartre, Paris, France 22–23
Moore, Henry 55
Mount Lycabettus, Athens, Greece 139
Mozart, Wolfgang Amadeus 55
Musée de l'Orangerie, Paris, France 17
Museu Nacional d'Art de Catalunya,
    Barcelona, Spain 80–81
Museum of Natural History, Vienna,
    Austria 188–189

Nagy, Imre 172
National Maritime Museum, Greenwich,
    London, England 33
Notre Dame, Paris, France 12–13

Oberbaum Bridge, Berlin, Germany 58–59

Palazzo Pitti, Florence, Italy 116–117
Paolozzi, Sir Eduardo 41
Parc del Laberint d'Horta, Barcelona,
    Spain 68–69
Parc Güell, Barcelona, Spain 74–75
Paris, France 11, 12–23
    Parc Montsouris 13
Parliament Building, Budapest,
    Hungary 174–175
Parthenon, Athens, Greece 136
Passage des Panoramas, Paris, France 21
Pennethorne, James 33
Peter Pan Statue, Kensington
    Gardens, London, England 25
Piazza San Marco, Venice, Italy 7, 122
Picasso, Pablo 17, 23, 76, 84
Piero della Francesca 114
Pittaki Street, Athens, Greece 132–133
Plaça Reial restaurants, Barcelona, Spain 73
Plato Sculpture, Trinity College,
    Dublin, Ireland 47
Poland 9
Ponte Vecchio on the River Arno,
    Florence, Italy 120–121
Portobello Road, London, England 24–25
Prague, Czech Republic 159, 160–169
    Prague Castle 6, 162–163
Pugin, Augustus 34
Puglieschi, Antonio 113
Pyramid of Cestius, Rome, Italy 106–107

Queluz National Palace, Lisbon,
    Portugal 90–91

Raphael 97, 108
Reichstag Building Cupola,
    Berlin, Germany 53
Reina Sofia Museum, Madrid, Spain 84
Rembrandt van Rijn 61, 114
Renoir, Pierre 17, 23
Rialto Bridge, Venice, Italy 124–125
Rijksmuseum, Amsterdam, The
    Netherlands 60–61
Roberts, Sir Gilbert 151
Rodríguez, Ventura 82
Roman Holiday 103
Rome, Italy 96–107

Roman ruins, Ostia Antica 98
Rona, Janoslav 164
Rossini, Gioachino 114
Rossio Square, Baixa District,
    Lisbon, Portugal 88
Royal Palace, Madrid, Spain 7, 86–87
Rumeli Fortress, Istanbul, Turkey 6, 156–157

Sade, Marquis de 18
Saint-Sulpice Church and Fountain,
    Paris, France 18–19
Salvi, Nicola 103
Samaria Gorge, Crete, Greece 143
Samuel Beckett Bridge, Dublin, Ireland
    7, 48–49
San Frediano in Cestello Church, Florence,
    Italy 112–113
Sanctis, Francesco de 103
Scala Contarini del Bovolo, Venice,
    Italy 124
Scandinavia 7–8
Schindler, Emil Jakob 181
Schönbrunn Palace, Vienna,
    Austria 182–183
Schubert, Franz 181
Scotch Whisky Experience,
    Edinburgh, Scotland 7, 39
Scott Monument, Edinburgh, Scotland
    36, 39
Shelley, Percy Bysshe 106
Sherlock Holmes Museum,
    London, England 30–31
Singel Canal, Amsterdam, The Netherlands
    64–65
Smirke, Sir Robert 44
Sobrino de Botín Restaurant,
    Madrid, Spain 7, 82
Sophocles 130
Spanish Steps, Rome, Italy 103
St Charles's Church, Vienna,
    Austria 180–181
St Giles Cathedral, Edinburgh,
    Scotland 36–37
St Paul's Cathedral, London,
    England 26–27
St Peter's Square, Rome, Italy 100–101
St Stephen's Basilica, Budapest,
    Hungary 178
St Stephen's Cathedral, Vienna,
    Austria 186–187
Statues in Memento Park,
    Budapest, Hungary 177
Steel, John 36
Steindl, Imre 174

Stephen's Green Shopping Centre,
    Dublin, Ireland 51
Stiassny, Wilhelm 164
Strauss, Johann 181
Strauss, Josef, II 181
Süleymaniye Mosque, Istanbul, Turkey 149
Sultan Ahmed Mosque, Istanbul,
    Turkey 152–153
Széchanyi Chain Bridge, Budapest,
    Hungary 178–179
Széchanyi Spa Baths, Budapest, Hungary 174

Temple Bar, Dublin, Ireland 46–47
Temple of Esculapio, Villa Borghese,
    Rome, Italy 104–105
Theatre of Dionysus, Athens,
    Greece 130–131
Tiepolo, Giambattista 86
Tiergarten, Berlin, Germany 55
Titian 97
Tower Bridge, London, England 28–29
Trastevere, Rome, Italy 7, 97
Trevi Fountain, Rome, Italy 102–103
tulips, Amsterdam Flower Market,
    Amsterdam, The Netherlands 61

Ucello, Paolo 114
Uffizi Gallery, Florence, Italy 114–115
UNESCO World Heritage Sites 28, 33, 74

Vajdahunyad Castle, Budapest,
    Hungary 171
Van Gogh, Vincent 23, 61
Vasari, Giorgio 114
Vatican City panorama, Rome,
    Italy 108–109
Velázquez Bosco, Ricardo 84
Velázquez, Diego 86
Venice, Italy 95, 122–129
Venus de Milo 17
Vermeer, Johannes 61
Vienna, Austria 159, 180–189
Vilaseca i Casanovas, Josep 76
Vivaldi, Antonio 187
Vrtbovská Garden, Prague, Czech
    Republic 160

Wellington Monument, Phoenix Park,
    Dublin, Ireland 44
Wiener Staatsoper, Vienna, Austria 184–185
Wren, Sir Christopher 26

Zola, Émile Nana 21